Battery Park City

Cities and Regions
Planning, Policy and Management

A series edited by Seymour J. Mandelbaum
University of Pennsylvania, Philadelphia

Volume 1
Battery Park City: Politics and Planning on the New York Waterfront
David L. A. Gordon

Forthcoming titles

Volume 2
Constructing Suburbs
Ann Forsyth

Volume 3
Rome's Planning Strategy
Franco Archibugi

Battery Park City

Politics and Planning on the New York Waterfront

David L. A. Gordon

Queen's University
Kingston, Ontario
Canada

Gordon and Breach Publishers

Australia   Canada   China   France   Germany   India   Japan
Luxembourg   Malaysia   The Netherlands   Russia   Singapore
Switzerland   Thailand   United Kingdom

Amsteldijk 166
1st Floor
1079 LH Amsterdam
The Netherlands

British Library Cataloguing in Publication Data

Gordon, David L. A.
    Battery Park City : politics and planning on the New York
    waterfront. — (Cities and regions : planning, policy and
    management ; v. 1)
    1. Waterfronts — New York (N.Y.)   2. Urban renewal — New York
    (N.Y.)   3. Urban renewal — Political aspects — New York
    (N.Y.)   4. Battery Park (New York, N.Y.)
    I. Title
    307.3′4′16′097471

ISBN   90-5699-558-8

A hundred times I have thought:
New York is a catastrophe,
and fifty times:
It is a beautiful catastrophe.

— Charles Edouard Jeanneret
Le Corbusier

(inscribed in the pavement of Battery Park City)

City of the world
(for all races are here,
all lands of the earth make contributions here):
City of the sea!
City of wharves and stores —
City of tall facades of marble and iron!
Proud and passionate mettle —
Some mad extravagant city!

— Walt Whitman

(engraved upon the railing of the Battery Park City Esplanade)

Contents

Illustrations

Introduction to the Series

Cities and Regions: Planning, Policy and Management is an international series of case studies addressed to students in programs leading to professional careers in urban and regional affairs and to established practitioners of the complex crafts of planning, policy analysis and public management. The series will focus on the work-worlds of the practitioners and the ways in which the construction of narratives shapes the course of events and our understanding of them. The international character of the series is intended to help both novice and experienced professionals extend their terms of reference, learning from "strangers" in unfamiliar settings.

Seymour J. Mandelbaum

Acknowledgments

The writing of this book was assisted by many people and organizations, but my primary intellectual debts must be to Alan Altshuler, Tony Gomez-Ibañez and Gary Hack, who guided me through my first comparative study of waterfront redevelopment. Bernard Frieden reviewed my initial thoughts on Battery Park City and Lynn Sagalyn introduced me to the public authorities literature and history of the Battery Park City Authority. Hok-Lin Leung, Mitchell Moss, Mohammad Qadeer and Andrejs Skaburskis provided insightful comments on earlier versions of the analysis.

Canada Mortgage and Housing Corporation was the primary sponsor, through a CMHC Scholarship. The Advisory Research Committee of Queen's University assisted in funding the 1995 fieldwork and publication preparation. Other financial support was provided by the Taubman Center for State and Local Government and the Graduate School of Design, both at Harvard University.

Almost thirty of Battery Park City's key participants agreed to be interviewed for this study, providing the foundation for the case research. The 1992 New York fieldwork was assisted by the Center for Urban Research at New York University, which made a wonderful base for research. Jon McMillian was my principal contact at the Battery Park City Authority and Robert Serpico supplied extensive data on the financial history of the agency. Max Abramovitz, Stanton Eckstut and James Rossant graciously allowed me to ransack their firm's archives for images of their plans for the project. The Downtown-Lower Manhattan Association also allowed me to search their files for important photographs and documents.

Wei Guo, Dino Melissa and Bill Tam improved the illustrations, while Ingrid Bron and Peter Linkletter provided valuable assistance by editing the manuscript.

Kirsty Mackay, my editor, was a constant source of good advice and encouragement throughout the publication process.

Finally, I owe this opportunity to Seymour Mandelbaum, whose comments have improved the story in many places.

Despite the wonderful help listed above, I take full responsibility for any errors or omissions in this study. However, it only seems fair to share any credit with my family and Katherine Rudder, who provided the best distraction of all by marrying me halfway through the writing.

INTRODUCTION

In October 1968, Governor Nelson Rockefeller and Mayor John Lindsay took a boat tour on the Hudson River to consummate their agreement on the development of Battery Park City. As they looked out at the rotting piers and landfill from the construction of the World Trade Center, they must have had visions of the modern urban project they would build on some of the most valuable real estate in the world. It had taken the pair two years to resolve their differences on Battery Park City, but progress was in sight at last. Expectations were high, now that money and the full weight of agreement of the state's powerful governor and the city's popular mayor were behind the project.

The two men were likely amazed and dismayed that no buildings arose for over a decade.

By 1996, Battery Park City was generally regarded as one of the most successful examples of urban waterfront redevelopment. It has been hailed as a triumph of urban design and a financial bonanza which funded affordable housing in New York's most needy neighborhoods. It was home to over 7000 residents, and 30,000 employees and thousands more people visited its splendid public spaces every day.

All of these benefits appeared as if by magic in the previous decade, but it is not generally understood that the project was conceived over thirty years earlier. As recently as 1979, its development authority faced bankruptcy and abandonment of the project, amid general dismay about its future.

Over the past three decades, the City and the State of New York have been directly engaged in the redevelopment of Battery Park City. Countless individuals, agencies and organizations have also been involved, but the Battery Park City Authority (BPCA) has been the central actor since the inception of the

1

project. As a result, the story of the renaissance of the Hudson
River waterfront in Lower Manhattan is a rich and complex one,
and can be told from several perspectives. This study presents an
overview of Battery Park's redevelopment from 1960 to 1995. It
focuses upon the experience of the central actor: the Battery Park
City Authority.

The agency's plans changed over time in reaction to new
urban design initiatives, changing political priorities and different market conditions. The study describes the sometimes painful
process of adjustment which has taken place over the years, in
response to these new conditions. Similarly, the changes in the
project financing are briefly examined; the project turned the
corner in the mid 1980's and is now regarded as a fiscal success
and as a source of revenue for affordable housing in New York
City. Finally, we will look at some of the current corporate structure and development issues for the future of Battery Park City.

The Battery Park City Site

Battery Park City has one of the world's most prominent sites:
the Hudson River waterfront at the tip of Manhattan (Figure 1).
It is part of the vista that astounded sea-borne visitors from Walt
Whitman to Le Corbusier as they passed the Statue of Liberty to
get their first glimpse of the towers of Manhattan rising from the
harbor (Figure 2). Although many visitors now arrive by air, the
postcard view remains an important icon of New York. Battery
Park City is an essential part of the urban ensemble around New
York Bay viewed daily by hundreds of thousands from the Staten
Island Ferry, the Verrazano Bridge or the great sweeping curve
into the Lincoln Tunnel.

For the residents of New York City, the ninety-two acre site is
perhaps best located by reference to the adjacent World Trade
Center and Financial District. The site had previously been occupied by cargo piers and ferry docks which had been abandoned
for some time.

The site is actually new land, since it was created by landfill
from 1967 to 1976. Extending lower Manhattan by landfill was
not a new idea. The tip of the island has expanded almost contin-
uously since 1650 (Figure 3). For the first three centuries, most
of the waterfront was devoted to shipping and industrial uses,

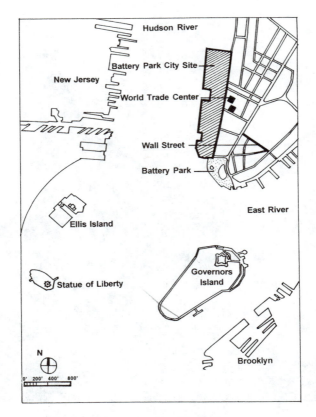

Figure 1 Battery Park City Site.
Source: Based on Cooper 1979.

while the fashionable residential districts were in the center of
the island. The Battery Park at the tip of Manhattan was one of
the few waterfront public spaces in the downtown. The new idea
was that the water's edge should be used for homes and offices
rather than shipping.

In the late nineteenth century, larger vessels and new technology permitted piers to be built on the lower Hudson River.
Manhattan was a busy port until after World War II, when the
Port Authority of New York and New Jersey built modern docks
at Port Elizabeth, New Jersey. With the advent of containerized

Figure 2   The Battery Park City Site in the 1990s.
Source: Downtown Lower Manhattan Association.

shipping, expressways and trucking in the 1960's, cargo activity in Lower Manhattan came to a standstill [Moss 1976; NYC OLMD 1975:5].

The New Jersey ferry and the ocean liner terminals also became obsolete as passengers switched to the trans-Hudson subways and expanded airports operated by the Port Authority. The abandoned piers began to decay and collapse, and they became a highly visible symbol of Lower Manhattan's decline in the early 1960's (Figure 4). By the late 1960's many agencies

Figure 3   Growth of Lower Manhattan Island by Landfill.
Source: Based on Wallace *et al.* 1965.

were examining how to make better use of New York's waterfront resources [Moss and Drennan 1976].

New York was not alone. The economic and technological
forces which made the lower Hudson piers obsolete were also
at work in most modern seaports from Tokyo to Rotterdam
[Bruttomesso 1993; 1991]. The new container ports required
large, vacant sites with good road and rail connections, so many
were built miles away from the inner city waterfront [Hoyle
et al., 1988]. The pace of change would be dramatic. Oakland

Figure 4   The Battery Park City Site in the 1960s.
Source: Battery Park City Authority.

eclipsed San Francisco five years after its new port opened, while the Port of London changed from the world's busiest harbour to Europe's largest redevelopment site in little more than a decade. The older port facilities were often located near the Central Business District and were tempting sites for urban redevelopment without the dislocation of the earlier urban renewal programs. These urban waterfront redevelopment projects became some of the most prominent examples of physical planning and urban renewal in the 1970's and 1980's [Breen and Rigby 1993]. New York simply got an early start in the worldwide urban waterfront phenomenon.

CHAPTER ONE

Duelling Plans: Proposals for the Lower Hudson Waterfront

Once it became obvious that the piers on the lower Hudson River were ripe for redevelopment, there was a scramble to initiate the project. Four separate groups prepared major proposals for its redevelopment from 1963–66:

1. the New York City Department of Marine and Aviation (DMA) which operated the existing piers.
2. the Downtown – Lower Manhattan Association (DLMA) led by David Rockefeller of the Chase Manhattan Bank.
3. the New York City Planning Commission (CPC), which has planning and land use authority.
4. the State of New York, with a personal interest by Governor Nelson Rockefeller.

The New York/New Jersey Port Authority was also active in the area, developing the massive World Trade Center on an adjacent site. It was strongly supported by David Rockefeller and the Downtown-Lower Manhattan Association as they attempted to stem the flow of office development to mid-town Manhattan [Danielson and Doig 1987:318]. The development agenda of each agency can be seen in their land use planning proposals. They used their plans as communications tools in the political debate over control of this high profile site.

Department of Marine and Aviation Plan

Since the City of New York owned the piers and land and regulated urban development, it might be expected that it would control redevelopment of the lower Hudson River waterfront. Indeed, the first major proposal for the site's development was

put forward by the New York City Department of Marine and
Aviation in April 1963 containing:

* six commercial pier slips
* eight office buildings
* eighteen high-rise apartment buildings with 4500 dwelling
  units
* a forty story hotel [Horne 1963]

The DMA study was led by Ebasco management consultants and
designed by Eggers and Higgins architects. The first phase of the
plan included landfill from the Battery Park to Chambers Street,
with apartments and offices built on top of a continuous 100 acre
complex of freight and slipping terminals (Figure 5). Subsequent
phases were to include a convention center and a new 'superliner' terminal to handle the substantial increase in maritime passenger traffic expected by the Department at that time.

The City's Department was now in the last stages of its strug-
gle for control of the Manhattan waterfront [NY CPC 1964]. It
was broke and wedded to an obsolete freight technology and to a
dream of continued high volumes of marine passenger traffic.
The ocean liner and general cargo freighter had been supplanted
by the jet aircraft and container ship. The Port Authority had
scooped them on both counts by building the container port and
taking over the region's airports. In addition, the Department's
plans for office buildings and industrial uses were opposed by
David Rockefeller and the DLMA. The Marine and Aviation
Department plan sank, but some parts were later salvaged by the
organizations which followed their lead.

The Department tried to hang onto the site again in November
1966, when it proposed a short takeoff and landing airport. This
proposal was also ignored. Ironically, the superliner terminal
was later completed and now sits almost unused near Midtown
Manhattan.

The Downtown-Lower Manhattan Association

The Downtown-Lower Manhattan Association was one of the
most powerful and effective private planning organizations in
New York during the 1950's and 1960's. David Rockefeller

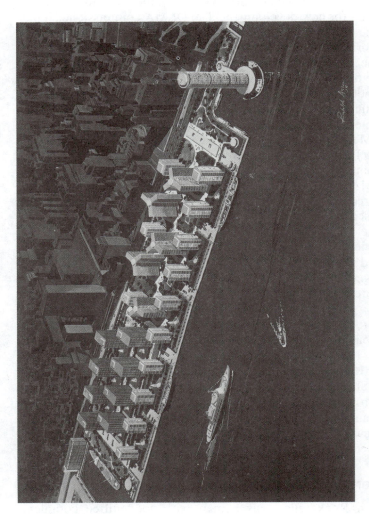

Figure 5 The New York City Department of Marine and Aviation 1963 Plan (Eggers and Higgins Architects).
Source: City of New York.

founded the organization in 1957, and showed leadership by
building a new bank headquarters at Chase Manhattan Plaza
during a period when Midtown Manhattan was the dominant
location for new development. The DLMA commissioned a plan
for the downtown area [DLMA 1958] and proposed that the Port
Authority build the World Trade Center.

The Department of Marine & Aviation proposal appeared
while the DLMA was revising its 1958 plan. They liked the idea
of landfill along the lower Hudson, but wanted a large residential
community adjacent to their office developments, without further
commercial competition. Their consultants, Skidmore, Owings
and Merrill, quickly changed their plan to include housing and
a hotel on the Hudson River and new buildings for the stock
exchange and a "world trade center" along the East River
[DLMA 1963; Wrubel 1995 interview]. Their plan (Figure 6)
was received cautiously by the press and City when it was
released in November 1963.

The DLMA's pressure for redevelopment of the area was
sufficiently powerful that Mayor Wagner's administration was
forced to respond. The City Planning Commission (CPC)
engaged a consortium of planning firms in February 1965 to
prepare a comprehensive plan for all of lower Manhattan. The
team was led by the Philadelphia planning firm Wallace McHarg
Roberts Todd with Wittlesey, Conklin and Rossant of New York
as urban designers. Their plan was expected to be completed in
early 1966, but a municipal election interrupted the process.
John Lindsay was elected Mayor in November 1965 on the
Republican ticket. The CPC released a draft version of the plan a
month later during the last week of the (Democratic) Wagner
administration. The final plan was delayed until the spring, while
the new mayor reviewed the proposals. In the meantime, the City
was scooped by the Governor.

Governor Rockefeller's Proposal – Battery Park City

Nelson Rockefeller was a man with an "edifice complex",
according to Brendan Gill. His first job was to lease the
Rockefeller Center and he also worked on the UN Headquarters
for his family before he entered politics. As New York State
Governor from 1959 through 1973, he built an astounding array

RECOMMENDED MAJOR IMPROVEMENTS

A. WORLD TRADE CENTER
B. NEW YORK STOCK
   EXCHNAGE
C. CIVIC CENTER
D. BROOKLYN BRIDGE
   SOUTHWEST
E. WASHINGTON STREET
   REDEVELOPMENT
F. HELIPORT
G. MARINA AND BOATEL
H. EAST RIVER ESPLANADE
I. HUDSON RIVER
   LANDFILL PROJECT
J. BROOKLYN BRIDGE
   SOUTHEAST
K. BROOKLYN BRIDGE NORTH

AERIAL VIEW OF LOWER MANHATTAN WITH INSET SKETCHES OF SEVERAL PROJECTS RECOMMENDED FOR FUTURE IMPROVEMENTS, INDICATED
BY LETTERS.   THE DOWNTOWN HELIPORT (F) WHICH HAS BEEN IN OPERATION FOR THE PAST THREE YEARS MAY BE EXPANDED IN SIZE AS
SHOWN ON THE MAP, IN MEETING THE NEEDS OF INCREASING TRAFFIC.

DOWNTOWN–LOWER MANHATTAN ASSOCIATION, INC

Figure 6   The Downtown Lower Manhattan Association 1963 Plan (Skidmore, Owings and Merrill).
Source: Downtown Lower Manhattan Association.

of projects – universities, hospitals, housing, office buildings, parks and the Albany Mall. Rockefeller was concerned about middle income housing in 1961 and established a study committee which proposed massive residential developments like Starrett City in Brooklyn and apartment buildings built on piers on the New York waterfront [Bleeker 1981: 114–16].

The Governor's interest in a residential development on the lower Hudson River waterfront probably emerged from the World Trade Center project. He had embraced the DLMA's proposal for a major office complex to consolidate firms engaged in foreign trade. The Governor directed the Port Authority to pursue it, since he was not pleased that New York had lost most of the container port traffic. The project immediately fell into trouble as New Jersey (the PA's other political master) opposed the East River site and wanted the offices to reinforce its trans-Hudson (PATH) subway. The two governors eventually agreed that the World Trade Center would be built over the PATH terminal on the Hudson River side, so that "New York would do the paperwork and New Jersey would carry the goods" [Lindquist 1995 interview].

The Port Authority's design team proposed that the fill from the mammoth excavation should be dumped into the river beside the site in 1965 (Figure 7). Nelson Rockefeller recognized the opportunity created by the proposed fill and City's delayed response to the DLMA's plan. He was determined to act in secret, since there was little development in downtown Manhattan in 1965 and it had been quite difficult to implement projects after the retirement of Robert Moses. Rockefeller's staff in Albany looked at the policy questions and the Governor retained his favorite architect, Wallace K. Harrison [Douglass; Lindquist 1995 interviews].

Harrison had earned the Governor's trust as a designer over a thirty year period, starting with the re-design of Rockefeller's apartment in 1934. However, his commission was clearly not favouritism, since Harrison would have been considered one of leading architects of his day [Newhouse 1989]. Harrison had previously built Rockefeller family houses, and worked on the design teams for Rockefeller Center, the 1939 World's Fair, and the UN. Nelson Rockefeller and Wallace Harrison were one of the most powerful client-architect relationships in recent

Figure 7   The World Trade Centre Under Construction with Landfill in the Hudson River.
Source: Downtown Lower Manhattan Association.

American history. Harrison was building the Albany Mall and Metropolitan Opera for the Governor when he was asked to prepare a plan for the lower Hudson River waterfront in late 1965.

Harrison's report was titled *Battery Park City: New housing space for New York*. The plan included:

- Housing for 13,982 families
- A hotel of 2200 rooms
- Two office buildings
- Public service facilities
- Recreation and shopping centers
- Light industrial facilities
- Parks and parking facilities [Harrison 1966:7]

Harrison's report was the first use of the name "Battery Park City" for the site. The idea of a "city within a city" was a current theme for the large master planned redevelopment projects of the 1960's. Battery Park City would share its last name with other New York public and private projects like Co-op City and Lefrak City.

The plan proposed housing for a mix of incomes and a wide range of community services. However, the design of the project left much to be desired. It consisted of rows of slab buildings on a pedestrian deck, over light industry. His partner, Max Abramovitz, later described it as "yesterday's kind of planning; a left over from Le Corbusier's ideas" (Figures 8 and 9). Harrison's biographer hinted that he might have been too busy on the Lincoln Center and Albany Mall to give the plan his complete attention [Newhouse 1989:164]. The office buildings shown in the renderings did seem similar to the Albany project.

Rockefeller unveiled the plan at a press conference on May 12, 1966, pre-empting the City's release of their plan. He achieved complete surprise and front page headlines with his secret initiative. Mayor John Lindsay's first glance at the plan was at the press conference (Figure 10): "That was the first time I saw the plan. I went to the press conference for political reasons, I didn't want to fight Nelson Rockefeller then." [Lindsay 1992 interview].

David Rockefeller was not at the press conference. Despite a decade of leadership in reviving Lower Manhattan, he only discovered his brother's plan when the DLMA staff showed him the newspaper that morning [Lindquist 1995 interview]. The Governor moved rapidly to mend fences with the DLMA by giving their executive a personal briefing three days later. However, *The New York Times*' Ada Louise Huxtable criticized the Governor's proposals for not being coordinated with the City and denounced Harrison's design [Huxtable 1966a & 1966b].

The New York City Planning Commission's Lower Manhattan Plan

The *Lower Manhattan Plan* [Wallace *et al.*, 1965] was finally released by the City Planning Commission in June 1966, a little over a month after the Governor's announcement. It was a comprehensive plan based upon a through review of land use and transportation south of Canal Street. Its recommendations included expansion of the financial core and residential development on

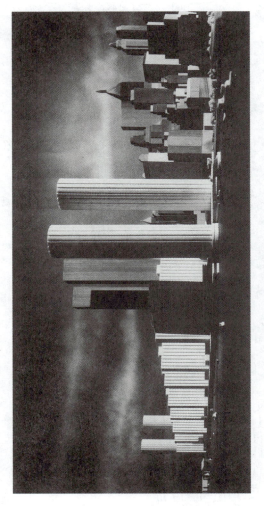

Figure 8 Model of Governor Rockefeller's 1966 Plan.
Photo: L. Checkman.
Source: Provided by Max Abramovitz.

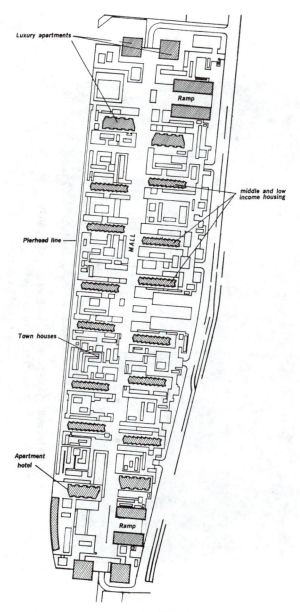

Figure 9   Governor Rockefeller's 1966 Plan.
Source: Harrison and Abramovitz 1966.

Figure 10   Nelson Rockefeller's Press Conference.
Photo: New York News.
Source: Arthur Wrubel.

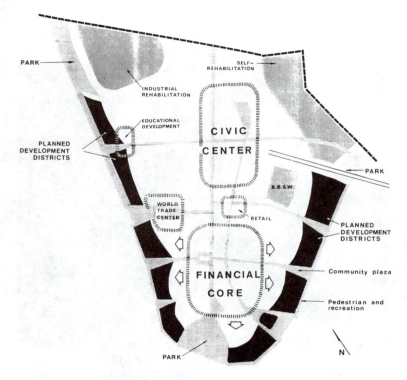

Figure 11 Lower Manhattan Plan Principles, 1966.
Source: Wallace *et al.* 1966.

landfill along the both Hudson and East River (Figure 11), following the broad strategy advocated by the DLMA.

The consulting team's urban design principles were described
by James Rossant:

> The main spatial idea was to create major corridors
> to the waterfront. Continuous and easy pedestrian
> access and "windows to the waterfront" were impor-
> tant objectives.
>
> The other important proposal was to weave in a
> new edge highway along the waterfront. It was to be
> depressed under the squares where the corridors met
> the water and on the surface in between. The existing
> West Street is a major barrier now. [Rossant 1992
> interview]

Like the DLMA scheme, the CPCs plan made extensive use of elevated platforms to separate vehicular and pedestrian circulation. The Lower Manhattan Plan was extensively illustrated with photographs, models, plans and some striking renderings of the East River (Figures 12, 13 and 14). It was enthusiastically received by the DLMA and the press [NYT editorial June 23,

Figure 12   East River Rendering from Lower Manhattan Plan, 1966.
Source: Lower Manhattan Plan.

Figure 13   East River Perspective.
Source: Lower Manhattan Plan.

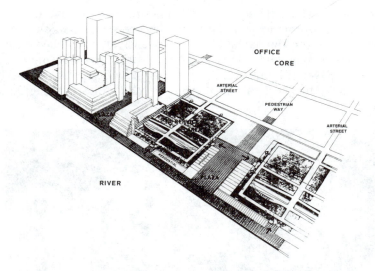

Figure 14 Multi Level Servicing, Lower Manhattan Plan, 1966.
Source: Lower Manhattan Plan.

1966]. The Lower Manhattan Plan also received immediate critical acclaim from the important architectural periodicals [Progressive Architecture 1966] and Ada Louise Huxtable:

> *The overall plan for the area ... is a powerful imaginative stimulant, demonstrating with sophisticated expertise New York's genuine potential as a beautiful and livable city of unparalleled dramatic excitement.... With this scheme, New York comes of planning age. [Huxtable 1966b].*

While the support of the design journals conferred professional prestige, an endorsement by *The New York Times*' Ada Louise Huxtable was a particular coup. She was not only the architectural design critic for the "paper of record"; she also sat on the paper's editorial board. Huxtable wrote many of the key editorials on urban projects. While a scathing review from the *Times*' drama critic could hurt a Broadway show, a bad review from their architecture critic could cause political problems for public or private developers.

The implementation proposals of the Lower Manhattan plan were rather vague. The report ends with a plea for a public development corporation:

> *Its function would be to plan and in some instances execute various portions of the development; in more instances however, it would be acting as agent for the city. The purpose of such an organization would be to provide a device for treating large segments as planned unit developments in order to insure the implementation of the plan's objectives. [Progressive Architecture 1966:132]*

New York City owned the land, had statutory power to regulate urban development and had prepared a superior plan. However, Nelson Rockefeller had the money, legislative authority and desire to build Battery Park City. Both parties agreed on the general policy – to develop a mainly residential community on landfill adjacent to the World Trade Center. However, they disagreed substantially on urban design and policy implementation.

A classic showdown between two public authorities ensued, and, of course, in the meantime, nothing was built.

CHAPTER TWO

The City and State Negotiate

The critical period for the launch of the Battery Park City project was the time between the Governor's announcement in May 1966 and the completion of the Master Development Plan and the execution of the Master Lease in 1969. The project could have disappeared, like many of the other Lower Manhattan waterfront schemes, except for the personal determination of Nelson Rockefeller to build it. In order to start the development, the Governor had to make an agreement with the new Lindsay administration, modify Harrison's plan, set up an implementation organization, arrange funding and obtain the necessary approvals for building.

Reaching Agreement with the City of New York

The negotiations between the Governor and the Mayor – both liberal Republicans and overtly political allies – might have been expected to go easily but they did not. Nelson Rockefeller had been one of John Lindsay's strongest supporters; providing not only visible support but also $500,000 in contributions to Lindsay's 1965 mayoral campaign [Wade 1990]. Unfortunately, the shared attitudes which brought them together in party politics did not carry through to the relations between the State and the City.

Lindsay arrived in City Hall as an "outsider" in a period of widespread concern about the City's finances and difficult labor relations [Netzer 1990:33]. He was immediately embroiled in strikes with civic employees and difficult negotiations with the State over his proposed city personal income tax. The Mayor adopted the symbols of a crusading reformer in his first term, as he attempted to build his own power base in the administration of the city. He established neighborhood city halls and established super-agencies based in the Mayor's office to gain control of issues [Eichenthal 1990:66–7].

The Governor was appropriating all the dramatic initiatives in urban development in Lower Manhattan: the World Trade Center, Battery Park City, the Second Avenue subway, the West Side Highway, etc. The Lindsay administration's response was to focus on the completion of the Lower Manhattan Plan and to build links to David Rockefeller's Downtown Lower Manhattan Association. The Governor had alienated his younger brother by not consulting him on a plan for an area where David had been working for over a decade. The DLMA supported the Lower Manhattan Plan when it was released [Carroll 1966].

Lindsay created the Office of Lower Manhattan Development (OLMD) in January 1967 to implement the Lower Manhattan Plan and work with the DLMA. The OLMD was controlled by the Mayor's office and first headed by Richard Buford and then Richard Weinstein, who both got along well with David Rockefeller [Elliot interview 1992].

When serious negotiations on Battery Park City began later in 1966, the City had improved its bargaining position by issuing its own plan for the entire Lower Manhattan area, getting support from the leading newspaper and business groups and establishing their own implementation authority. The negotiations were not easy; they involved numerous meetings at the Governor's office on 55th Street. In addition, each team brought their design consultants: Conklin and Rossant (C & R) for the City and Harrison and Abramovitz (H & A) for the State.

It took the City and State three years to work out their differences. Four major issues were involved:

- The financial return to the city.
- The proportion of low income housing units.
- The design of the project.
- The arrangements for continuing city participation in project implementation.

The basic irritation underlying the entire negotiation was whether the State should control the redevelopment of City-owned property. In the end, the two parties made a trade: the state would develop BPC, while the City would get the Governor's support for a proposed Linear City project over a Brooklyn expressway [Elliot interview 1992]. The City and the DLMA took the initiative on several other projects on the East River waterfront, leaving the state to deal with the lower Hudson.

The money issue was solved by the state agreeing that the proposed Battery Park City Authority (BPCA) would pay the City ground rent and payments in lieu of taxes. It was also agreed that New York City would also receive any surplus of revenue over expenditures, should the agency ever begin to show a profit in the future.

Mayor Lindsay wanted all the housing to be tax-paying luxury apartments, arguing that the valuable sites would generate money that could be used for low-income housing elsewhere. Governor Rockefeller wanted a fifty percent luxury / forty percent middle-income / ten percent low-income split. City Planning Commission chairman Donald Elliot doubted the suitability of the area for family housing:

> Low income housing at Battery Park City did not seem to us to be a sensible thing to do. There were limited services for residents in Lower Manhattan, few schools, shops or social services. The project would probably get young people, singles and couples who worked downtown. [Elliot 1992 interview]

The DLMA supported the City's position. Their 1958 and 1963 plans recommended that low and middle income housing be located in several projects north of Battery Park City. The first was the redevelopment of the old Washington Street wholesale food market, immediately north of the BPC site, which was replaced by the Independence Plaza project and the Manhattan Community College. The second downtown moderate income project was Southbridge Towers, east of City Hall. The DLMA suggested that the BPC site had the best potential for market housing, since residents would enjoy spectacular waterfront views and could easily walk to work in the Financial District. The DLMA reinforced its position by retaining James Felt, a leading real estate consultant, and presenting the Mayor and Governor with a market study which reinforced their views. This

report was the first market research of the Battery Park City proposal and Felt later became the BPCA's residential consultant.

The initial compromise in the housing issue was that two
thirds would be conventional and one third assisted. This
arrangement did not survive the city's approvals process.

The detailed design of the complex project could not be settled
by negotiation between politicians. The two sides agreed to a
design process with a panel consisting of the governor's architect
(Harrison), the City's architect (C & R) and Philip Johnson as a
third party mediator. This agreement put the complicated design
issues on hold, to be worked out after the political and financial
issues were resolved.

The final problem area was continuing City participation in
the implementation of a project developed by a State agency. The
State agreed to involve the City in the design of the plan, to
attach a detailed master development plan to the lease and refer
all projects to an Architectural Review Board set up by the City
to examine each development proposal. Lindsay and Rockefeller
signed a memorandum of understanding on these points in April,
1968.

Designing the New Plan

Mayor Lindsay had made it clear from the beginning of the
negotiations that Harrison's design for Battery Park City was
unacceptable [Lindsay 1992 interview]. Philip Johnson was
therefore engaged for the delicate task of mediating between
the Governor's architect and personal friend, and Conklin and
Rossant, the City's urban designers. Johnson was ideally quali-
fied for the job, as a leading architect with personal ties to both
Lindsay and Rockefeller. He had taken Lindsay on a well publi-
cized helicopter tour of the city during the mayoral campaign to
discuss new urban initiatives. Johnson also had a long-standing
relationship with the Rockefeller family through his forty year
involvement with the Museum of Modern Art [Johnson interview
1992].

The three firms established a project office in space provided
by the Governor in the RCA building at Rockefeller Center. The

mezzanine offices had previously been used by Harrison, Rockefeller and a group of international architects to design the UN headquarters. The new planning team included a small group of architects and urban designers drawn from the C & R and H & A firms. James Rossant and William Conklin dropped in to the project office every day for an hour or two. They would also meet Philip Johnson for lunch every week at the Four Seasons restaurant (which Johnson designed) before joining Wallace Harrison (and occasionally Max Abramovitz) at the project office to review the latest work.

The principal designers also briefed Nelson Rockefeller at his Manhattan townhouse. The Governor maintained his strong interest in the project, and was particularly taken with the idea of clustering the offices at the south end and providing a shopping mall which connected it to the center of the site. James Rossant produced two definitive perspective views of these ideas, working at the office, and drawing into the night at his own home:

> Those drawings really got the City excited about the project. We modified the Lower Manhattan Plan for the area by gridding the pods and making a more regular disposition of buildings. We kept the plazas and the access to the water. [Rossant interview 1992]

It took less than a year for the team to produce a plan that was satisfactory to both the Governor and the City. They joined the office node from Harrison's plan to the residential pods from Conklin and Rossant. Philip Johnson spent considerable time with the Governor working on the view of the new office complex at the tip of Manhattan [Johnson 1992 interview]. The design was unveiled at a news conference in April 1969, complete with futuristic renderings by Rossant, models and enthusiastic comments from both the Mayor and Governor.

The critical response was supportive. Ada Louise Huxtable concluded her review with "In this any way to plan a city? You bet it is" [Huxtable 1969]. *Architectural Record* described it as "a proposal for new housing, new jobs, and new land ... perhaps a new kind of urban life" [Jensen 1969]. The rendering of the

Figure 15   Rendering of 1969 City/State Plan (Conklin and Rossant; Harrison and Abramovitz; Philip Johnson). *Source:* Battery Park City Authority (Rendering by J. Rossant).

new plan (Figure 15) later appeared in many publications. It seemed to catch the spirit of the Space Age, during the year when the United States landed a man on the moon. Battery Park City was the City of the Future.

Setting up the Battery Park City Authority

Once the preliminary agreement was reached with the City, Rockefeller took the first steps to implement the project. The State of New York made extensive use of special purpose authorities to implement its development program in the 1960's [Walsh 1990], and Rockefeller selected Charles J. Urstadt, NYS Deputy Commissioner of Housing and Community Renewal, to head the agency he proposed to build the Battery Park City. Urstadt helped draft the legislation:

> *I looked at several agencies' mandates when we were writing the legislation, including the Port Authority and [Robert Moses] Triborough Bridge Authority; there were lots of examples then ... I wanted the right to offer tax-exempt, moral make-up bonds.*
>
> *Board members were to have six year terms so they would outlast any Mayor or Governor. I also wanted as few Board members as possible and administrative independence, to avoid interference ... I only wanted jurisdiction for the area we were going to build, otherwise people oppose you for proposals off your site. [Urstadt interview 1992]*

The legislation establishing the Battery Park City Corporation Authority was approved in May 1968. The Authority consists of three members appointed by the Governor, for six year terms. The statement of purpose for the Authority found that the site was a blighted area and declared that its redevelopment was in the public interest:

> *... the replanning, reconstruction and redevelopment of such area including the filling of the Hudson River at such area up to the present pierhead line, the preparation of the resulting land for development, and the creation in such area, in cooperation with the city*

Figure 16 Governer Rockefeller Unveiling the 1969 Plan with Battery Park City Authority Board Member A.S. Mills and Chairman Charles Urstadt. *Source*: Battery Park City Authority.

> *of New York and the private sector, of a mixed commercial and residential community, with adequate utilities systems and civic and public facilities such as schools, open public spaces, recreational and cultural facilities, is necessary for the prosperity and welfare of the people of the city of New York and of the state as a whole ... [NYS* General Laws 1968, *c.343]*

The authority was specifically authorized to issue bonds "for any corporate purpose." Later amendments to the Act limited the amount of the bonds to $300 million [NYS *General Laws. 1971*, c.377] and changed the name of the agency to the Battery Park City Authority [NYS *General Laws. 1969*, c.624].

Charles Urstadt was elected Chairman of the BPCA in August 1968 and guided the agency for over a decade (Figure 16).

Getting the Approvals

The final steps in consummating the agreements between the City and the State were approval of the Master Development

Plan by the City Planning Commission (CPC) and the Board of Estimate (B of E) and execution of a lease for the property from the City to the State. The political negotiations and redesign had taken so long that the agreements had to be approved during the city election campaign of 1969.

John Lindsay was in a vulnerable position, since he lost the Republican nomination in the primary and was running solely on the Liberal ticket. The Democrats were running Mario Procaccino, a "law and order" candidate, against him and Lindsay needed the support of the liberal wing of the Democratic party [Hamilton 1990:370]. Percy E. Sutton, a prominent Harlem politician, was running a successful campaign for Manhattan borough president. Sutton demanded changes in the mix of housing as a condition for supporting the plan at the CPC and Board of Estimate [Lindsay interview 1992]. Other interest groups including the Urban League and the Women's City Club attacked the plan at the CPC hearings in July.

To bolster the campaign for City approvals, the BPCA ran large newspaper advertisements during the summer seeking interest in living in the site. The ad received thousands of responses, which were used in the debate by the BPCA's supporters. However, by mid-August Lindsay was forced to change his position to support a housing mix of one-third low income, one-third middle income and one-third market housing. The plan was approved at the CPC in August, 1969 by a vote of four to one [NYC CPC-20789].

The Master Lease for the site was then approved by the Board of Estimate in October 1969, at the last meeting before the municipal election. The lease was set for ninety-nine years starting in 1970, when construction was expected to begin. The City was to receive the net revenue of the BPCA after expenses, revenues and department service. The BPCA agreed to a schedule which completed the site improvements by 1978 and the housing by 1983.

Battery Park City had a site, an approved plan, an implementation agency with authority to raise capital, and the political consensus on what needed to be done.

No buildings would rise for over ten years.

CHAPTER THREE

The 1969 Master Development Plan

The program for the 1969 master development plan was specified in the Master Lease with the City of New York. It required
the agency to build:

- five million square feet of offices
- 14,100 apartments (evenly split among high, moderate and
  low-income)
- a 500,000 square foot shopping center
- 27.5 acres of parks
- civil facilities including two schools, a library, police and fire
  stations
- a health center and a culture and recreation center
  [BPCA 1972:8]

In addition to these program elements, the BPCA was also
required to construct all the utilities, streets and a separate pedestrian circulation mall above most of the site.

Physical Design

The 1969 Master Development Plan specifically envisioned a
megastructure, a single building complex quite different from the
remainder of the Manhattan building fabric. The megastructure
was to be tied together by an enclosed seven story spine which
would run the entire length of the site (Figure 17). The spine
would incorporate retail, community facilities and a suspended
"people-mover."

Seven development pods would plug into the megastructure.
The commercial pod, located at the south end of the site, would

Figure 17   Inside the Spine of the 1969 Plan.
Source: Battery Park City Authority (Rendering by J. Rossant).

consist of a ten story commercial podium with three office towers of sixty, fifty, and forty stories respectively above this level (Figure 18). The Empire State Building and World Trade Center would have been the only taller buildings in the world at that time. Governor Rockefeller was particularly enthusiastic about placing the offices at the south end, where they would have dramatic views of the harbor and would present a strong image; he called it "the best spot in town" [Douglass 1995; Johnson 1992 interviews]. The World Trade Center was just starting construction, and it seems clear that its impact upon the downtown office market and transit accessibility were not fully understood in 1968, since both the client and the designers assumed that land values would be highest at the southern tip of Manhattan.

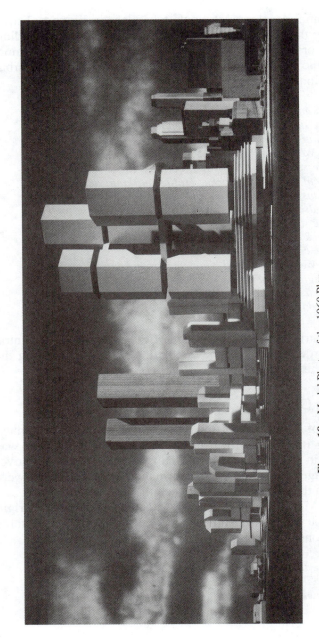

Figure 18 Model Photo of the 1969 Plan.
(Conklin and Rossant; Harrison and Abramovitz; Philip Johnson).
Photo: L. Checkman
Source: J. Rossant.

Residential development would take place in six pods distributed along the spine. Each pod would contain a service podium and four or five attached slab buildings (Figure 19). James Rossant, the principal designer of the plan, described the urban design rationale for the pods:

> We intended that "the pedestrian would be King" in the area, with roads diverted under the main pedestrian squares.
> We coined the term "pods" for the sites between the squares. These would be huge areas of development, like superblocks. Traffic, parking, access and transfers of level would take place in the base of the pods, while the road would simply go straight under the square. The development would take place on the deck on top, which would be tied back to the rest of the city at the elevation of Broadway ...
> We were not really interested in big complexes by a single architect. We just believed that in high density areas, you have to integrate highways, transit and parking. [Rossant interview 1992]

The megastructure required that the BPCA pre-build the central spine in order to provide the circulation system connecting the pods and the rest of the city.

Planning Controls

The City of New York officials did not trust the development agency to implement the Master Plan in the form that was designed in 1969. The Master Development Plan and over twenty pages of detailed performance specifications were attached to the Master Lease between the City and the State.

The OLMD planners later confided that they wanted a rigid plan so that when the Authority came back for the inevitable modifications they would be in a better bargaining position:

> The then director of Lower Manhattan Development for the City, Richard Buford, wrote into the lease between the Battery Park City Authority and the City provisions that the site plan must be followed exactly.

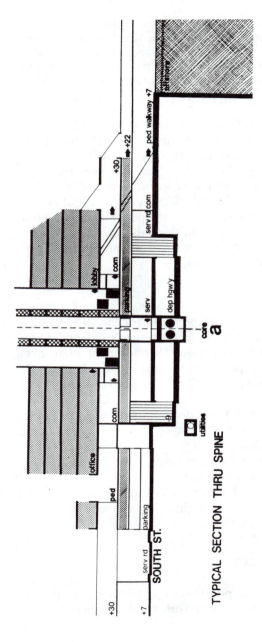

Figure 19 Cross Section of the 1969 Spine.
Source: J. Rossant.

> *A capable and experienced administrator, Buford*
> *knew that, while appearing to relinquish all rights to*
> *interfere in the design of the project, he was actually*
> *retaining full control for the City. It was inevitable*
> *that the lease would have to be renegotiated. [Barnett*
> *1974:58)*

The planners did not have to wait long. The BPCA requested modifications to the plan in 1974, following their first cost analysis. By this time, the City planners had completed the Lower Manhattan Waterfront Plan and were alarmed by the way the spine would cut views to the water along existing streets (NYC OLMD, 1975, p. 37). The city permitted the BPCA to convert its enclosed spine to an open mall, provided it was cut at the major streets. In addition, the technical appendix to the Master Lease was replaced with twenty-three pages of closely printed zoning regulations.

Cost Estimates

The first cost estimates prepared for the BPCA indicated that it would be extraordinarily expensive to carry out the public works associated with the Master Development Plan, even with the open mall concept rather than the enclosed spine. The development costs were estimated at over $240 million:

– site acquisition and development	$62.4 million
– utilities	$14.1 million
– civil facilities	$40.5 million
– streets, bridges, open space and pedestrian circulation	$58.3 million
– foundations for public facilities	$19.2 million
– architectural and engineering services	$26.0 million
– contingency (10%)	$22.1 million
Total	$242.6 million

[BPCA 1972:C-47]

The BPCA was responsible for construction of all of these facilities, but the City of New York would be responsible for maintenance of streets, roads, pedestrian areas, and public open space. The Master Lease required the BPCA to commence construction of the civic improvements in 1975 and complete them all by June 1983.

Plan Implementation

The detailed implementation process by which the BPCA would arrange to have a revenue-producing building constructed was not clearly evident from the Master Development Plan or the Master Lease. However, a review of BPCA documents implies the following process:

1. BPCA designs service spine.
2. BPCA submits service spine design to Permanent Architectural Review Board (PARB) for review and approval.
3. BPCA submits amendments to the Master Development Plan (MDP) (if required) to the CPC for review and approval.
4. CPC submits amendments to the Board of Estimate for review and approval.
5. BPCA commences construction of the service spine.
6. BPCA selects a master developer for a pod.
7. Pod developer designs common platform.
8. BPCA reviews pod platform design and connections to service spine.
9. Pod developer designs towers.
10. BPCA approves total design.
11. Pod design sent to PARB for review and approval.
12. Amendments to Master Development Plan submitted to CPC (if needed).
13. Amendments to MDP submitted to Board of Estimate (if necessary.
14. Developer builds complete platform.
15. Developer builds first individual tower.

The BPCA and the City of New York recognized that this process was unwieldy. The Permanent Architectural Review Board was eliminated in favor of the BPCA conforming to the detailed special zoning district provisions adopted in 1973.

Neither the City Planning Commission nor the Board of Estimate would review individual projects if they precisely conformed to this complicated ordinance. The City planners, who were still trying to change the BPCA plan, counted upon the inevitable amendments for future negotiating leverage.

CHAPTER FOUR

Getting Started

The first decade of the BPCA began with optimism and limited results. Demolition of the dilapidated piers which had been featured in the approvals process began in July 1970 and was completed before the fill permits were obtained. The Battery Park City site started with 24.7 acres already filled from the WTC excavations. The PATH subway tubes going to the WTC required the adjacent six acres to be built as an expensive platform over the tubes. The remaining sixty-five acres of land were created by hydraulic fill behind a new seawall. Millions of cubic yards of sand were dredged up from the bottom of Lower New York Bay and carried to the site in the barge that would pump it behind the new bulkhead. When the fill was completed in 1976, the Battery Park City site was a vacant sandy lot at the foot of the World Trade Center.

The cost of creating the site was estimated at $42.6 million in the BPCA's original land prospectus [BPCA 1972], or about $12 per square foot for the eighty-five acres of new land, excluding utilities. The land cost was quite attractive when compared to Manhattan real estate, which was valued at perhaps $200 per square foot at the time.

Designating Developers

The New York City real estate market was in its strongest period of post-war growth (up to that time) when Battery Park City was approved in 1969. Newspaper stories ran headlines like "How to Love the Boom" [Huxtable 1969a]. By the time the BPCA was ready to issue bonds, the sheer volume of the vacant space and projected construction was a cause for concern, especially the impact of the World Trade Center's nine million square feet of new office space. Another ten million square feet were completed on the east side of the downtown between 1968 and 1973 [DLMA 1973]. The Authority's own office market consultants, James D. Landauer and Associates, were concerned about the drop in absorption of new office space since 1971, and could not predict that the Battery Park City offices could be leased any earlier than January 1976 [BPCA 1972:32].

The initial response from the private sector was not encouraging. The BPCA ran advertisements for prospective office leases from September to December 1970 with fairly meager results. The Authority then switched tactics and began to solicit interest from the few private developers big enough to build the six million square foot office pod in the Master Development plan. This approach had more success, when BPCA announced that Harry Helmsley was designated as the office developer for the site in early 1972.

Helmsley owned one of the country's largest real estate portfolios including the Empire State Building and Tudor City in New York. (His new hotel, the Park Lane, on Central Park South was his first foray into the hotel business, for which he and his wife later became notorious). The front page coverage of his designation in *The New York Times* and an announcement in the May 1972 land prospectus must have given some comfort to potential investors, even though Helmsley had not entered into any legal agreements at the time. In fact, Richard Kahan later noted that the designation was little more than Helmsley tying up the site for no significant outlay, while waiting for market conditions to improve [Kahan interview 1992].

The residential picture looked brighter in the early 1970's, as ample state and federal funding was available for low and moderate income housing. The Mitchell-Lama housing program was producing large middle income residential projects like Starrett City and Co-op City elsewhere in New York. The federal government was providing funds for public housing and senior citizen housing in considerable quantities. The outlook for luxury rental housing was more cautious, according to James Felt & Company, the BPCA's market analyst: they believed that the market for luxury rental apartments in lower Manhattan was about 6000 units. Felt assessed that Battery Park City could market 4700 units if there was little significant competition in the area, including the City of New York's proposed Manhattan Landing project on the East River [BPCA 1972:35].

The BPCA advertised for residential developers in April 1971. In the 1972 land prospectus it was stated that the BPCA had interviewed over twenty prospective developers, was engaged in preliminary negotiations with three, and "It was anticipated by the Authority that a developer or developers for these neighborhoods will be selected within sixty days" [BPCA 1972:16]. The BPCA actually signed a letter of intent with the Lefrak Organization and Fisher Brothers during the next year. Lefrak was New York's largest residential builder and one of the few who could build on the scale demanded by the 2000 unit pods in the 1969 plan. He specialized in systems-built, low and middle income housing, such as the rather monotonous Lefrak City in Queen's. Richard Kahan, who worked for Lefrak on the BPC project, recalls that this letter of intent was also a mechanism to get a major developer involved with very little up-front investment [Kahan interview 1992].

Funding the Authority

Charles Urstadt's first move as BPCA Chairman was to obtain two loans totaling $600,000 from the Chase Manhattan Bank and Morgan Guarantee Trust Company. The loans were used to set up the BPCA office and to pay consultants' fees for engineering and site planning. Urstadt then negotiated a $15 million line of credit from the State in July 1969 [BPCA 1972:58]. They only used $5 million to keep the BPCA going until 1972.

The most important financial move in the first 10 years of the BPCA was Urstadt's decision to go to the bond market in 1972, even though all the funds were not immediately required:

> *Arthur Levitt, the State controller, only wanted to do $50 million at first, but we had authorization to $300 million. I convinced Goldman Sachs and Kuhn Loeb that we could do $200 million, which we sold in 1972. [Urstadt interview 1992]*

The bonds were successfully marketed on May 1, 1972. The issue included $45.2 million in serial bonds (at 4.8 to 6%) maturing over the period 1980–85 and $154.8 million in term bonds (at 6–3/8%) due in 2014 [BPCA 1972].

The bond prospectus was supported by the office and residential market studies and project cost estimates prepared by engineering consultants. However, the most important financial plan was the development schedule, which called for a rapid build out of the project. The six million square feet of offices were assumed to be occupied between 1976 and 1979 and the 14,000 apartments to be leased between 1975 and 1981. The development schedule was translated into estimated cash flows from leases which escalated from $8 million in 1976 to over $32 million annually by 1980, in order to pay off the bonds [BPCA 1972:51].

The $200 million bond issue generated $141.8 million in cash for the BPCA's use. The remainder was set aside for capitalized interest, reserves and the costs of the bond issue. The agency used $5 million of the cash to repay the State's line of credit [BPCA 1972:18] and spent another $45 million to create the landfill. The remaining cash of $90 million was not enough to build the seven story spine called for in the plan, so it was kept in the bank while the BPCA pursued private investment. The BPCA rode out the 1974–79 New York financial crisis on this bank balance. Despite interest rates rising dramatically in the late 1970's, the return on this fund only covered about half the annual $19.5 million debt service on the bonds, and the BPCA's financial position would deteriorate rapidly if development was stalled.

The capitalized interest fund created from the bond proceeds would pay the bondholders while the BPCA had no revenue coming in during the site development schedule assumed in the plan. The bonds' reserve fund provided a cushion of one or two years if construction or leasing was slower than the schedule assumed during the boom years of the early 1970's. The agency needed the developers to start building by the mid-1970's or it would have trouble meeting its bond obligations.

Finally, Urstadt secured further funding when he obtained authorization from New York State to borrow $400 million in mortgage backed bonds under the Mitchell-Lama housing program. The BPCA was able to use this authorization in

1980–84 to float $115.9 million in Housing Revenue bonds for Gateway Plaza at a time when very little funding for middle income housing subsidies was available.

Fencing with the City

The BPCA's relationship with the City of New York grew more difficult in the early 1970's. The competition started at the top, where John Lindsay was pursuing the Democratic nomination for President, while Nelson Rockefeller was seeking the Republican endorsement for the nation's highest political office. The Governor appointed Mario Procaccino, Lindsay's opponent in the mayoral election, to the BPCA Board. Locally, the Mayor and DLMA were actively pushing the Manhattan Landing and South Street Seaport projects on the East River, while Battery Park City was clearly identified as Governor Rockefeller's project. Urstadt noted "We were the State coming onto their land and they resented it; we were occupying troops in hostile territory" [Urstadt interview 1992]. He saw Manhattan Landing as serious competition for BPC and objected informally and formally.

The bureaucratic skirmishing between the BPCA and the City intensified. The City pursued its own planning agenda for the Lower Manhattan through the Office of Lower Manhattan Development. Their staff prepared the Lower Manhattan Waterfront Plan in 1974 (Figure 20), which included new urban design controls, such as view corridors down the main streets to the water (Figure 21). The planners attacked the spine of Battery Park City's megastructure through a series of negotiations with the BPCA over amendments to the Master Development Plan and the Master Lease. The Authority needed amendments to adjust the housing mix to what their advisors could support for the bond prospectus (thirty percent luxury, fourteen percent low income). The BPCA also wanted to get rid of the overly detailed planning and implementation regulations in the Master Lease. The City agreed to abolish the Permanent Architectural Review Board. The BPCA in turn agreed to submit to detailed special zoning district provisions. Individual projects would not have to be reviewed by the City Planning Commission or City Board of Estimate if they completely conformed to all the provisions of

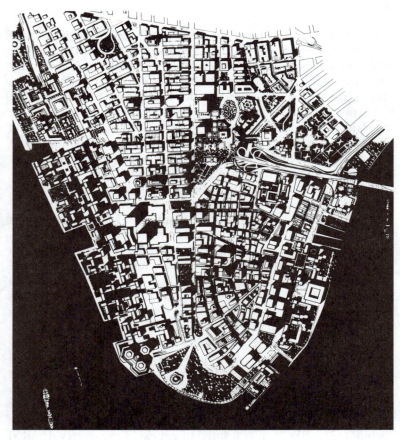

Figure 20   Lower Manhattan Waterfront Plan.
Source: Office of Lower Manhattan Development, 1975.

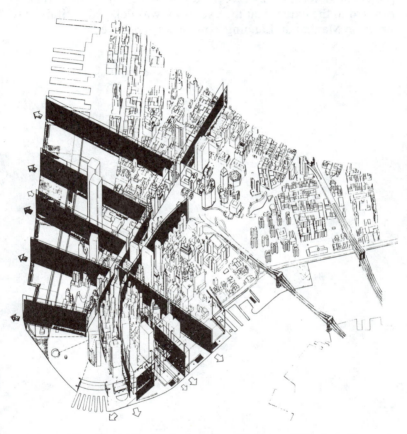

Figure 21 View Corridors in the Lower Manhattan Waterfront Plan.
Source: Office of Lower Manhattan Development, 1975.

this new zoning ordinance. Any amendments, however, would require full review and approval.

Urstadt eventually withdrew his objections to Manhattan Landing in exchange for an extension of the Battery Park City project area north to Jay Street. Relations with the City had deteriorated to the extent that the extension was delayed until the day *after* the Manhattan Landing Zoning was approved.

CHAPTER FIVE

Stalling Out: 1972–79

The Battery Park City Authority's progress came to an abrupt halt after the bond issue and the landfill were completed. Three major problems emerged in the mid-1970's: the rigid and complex Master Development Plan could not be implemented, there was no market for the office space, and both the City and the State had a fiscal crisis which paralyzed their development agencies.

Revising the Master Development Plan

After the Master Development Plan was approved by the City, the BPCA released its three distinguished architects and engaged an engineering firm to develop detailed drawings and cost estimates for implementation. This move drew a withering review from *The New York Times*: "How Not to Build a City" [Huxtable 1970] and lost its editorial support for most of the decade.

The engineers quickly determined that the spine was extraordinarily expensive, and would have to be built by the Authority before private development could begin. They began to explore ways to build the spine incrementally. Meanwhile, the market analysis of the plan indicated that retail development should be consolidated in a shopping center enclosed by two department stores, rather than spread out along the spine [BPCA 1972:36].

The new residential developers, Lefrak and Fisher, first retained Moshe Safdie, architect of the prefabricated Habitat apartment complex at Expo '67, to prepare a new design (Figure 22), but quickly dropped the idea. They then put their in-house architects to work simplifying the BPCA's pod design to fit Lefrak's standard construction systems. The City's Office of Lower Manhattan Development was dismayed by the drawings it began to see. The planners also had new urban design objectives from their Lower Manhattan Waterfront Plan. They put pressure

49

Figure 22   Lefrak and Fisher's Habitat Plan (Moshe Safdie).
Source: Moshe Safdie and Associates.

on the State through the DLMA, and the BPCA retained Wallace
Harrison's partner, Max Abramovitz as an architectural consultant in 1973 [Abramovitz interview 1992].

The residential pod scheme was developed further, respecting
the City's new planning criteria and view corridors. The retail
was consolidated from the spine into one 500,000 square foot
shopping center. Lefrak and Urstadt were quite concerned about
residential safety at the time, and Oscar Newman's "defensible
space" concepts were highly visible [Newman 1973]. The new
pod designs were like a fortress with a single guarded entrance,
and a second level pedestrian deck separated from the access and
service below (Figure 23). Abramovitz attempted to keep the
basic concepts of the Master Development Plan, but there were
constant conflicts with Lefrak and his in-house architects over
the plan and quality of the public spaces [Goldberger 1974:41].
In effect, Abramovitz was attempting to carry out urban design
review without the proper authority or even agreement over the
nature of the plan to be implemented. In the end Abramovitz
resigned, after the BPCA made him responsible to the developers, rather than the agency itself [Abramovitz interview 1992].

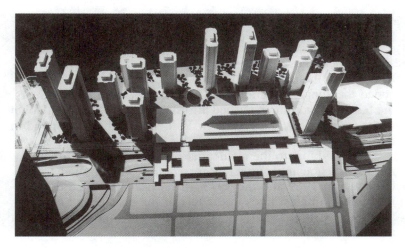

Figure 23 Lefrak and Fisher's Pod III (Harrison and Abramovitz). *Photo*: Checkman Photo. *Source*: Harrison and Abramovitz.

The Real Estate Market Collapse

The office space oversupply did not seem insurmountable at first when Henry Helmsley was announced as Battery Park City's office developer. However, the World Trade Center glutted the downtown market just as the economy contracted. The office market collapsed for a decade.

Not only did office supply collapse, but employment also declined sharply from 1972 to 1975, as New York City even lost office jobs. The combination of vacant space and declining demand sent Manhattan office rents tumbling down. Cushman and Wakefield observed a decline in average asking rent from $13.00 per square foot in 1970 to $7.00 in 1973. Rents did not recover to their nominal 1970 levels until the end of the decade [BPCA 1990b:C-2].

Residential development fared no better than offices. Plans to finance the middle-income housing at Battery Park City with housing revenue bonds were put on hold when the Urban Development Corporation defaulted on a bond obligation in 1975. Instead, the BPCA applied for federal assistance in the form of

FHA mortgage insurance. Unfortunately, federal officials were preoccupied with other projects and the insurance did not arrive until 1980, over five years after the routine approval was sought.

The federal government was the traditional source of funds for low income housing, but the Nixon administration effectively ended the supply programs in 1973. For the next twenty years, the federal government pushed affordable housing funding down to the state and local levels. New York was unable to respond in the 1970's.

The final blow to the residential program was the collapse of the luxury housing market. Rent control was applied to new buildings in 1969 and the 1973–75 recession stopped development. High interest rates in the rest of the decade and concerns about the City's fiscal crisis kept private construction to a minimum.

The New York City Fiscal Crisis

The long economic boom in New York City ended after Battery Park City was approved in 1969. The City's spending had grown rapidly in the 1960's and its revenues began to lag behind. During the recession in the early 1970's, the City began to add short term debt and conceal the size of its deficit [Netzer 1990:42]. The problem was not just the recession – the underlying economy of New York was undergoing dramatic change with the loss of manufacturing and the flight of office jobs from the City. New York lost over 500,000 jobs from 1970 to 1977.

In March 1975, the bond market was closed to the City and its fiscal crisis was in full flight. The State appointed the Municipal Assistance Corporation (MAC) to help get the City back into the bond market, but the initial cuts were not enough to balance the municipal budget. The State then established the Emergency Fiscal Control Board (EFCB) and gave it unprecedented powers over the City's finances. EFCB approval was required for all budgets, contracts, expenditures and borrowings [Bellush and Netzer 1990:313].

The BPCA was placed under the supervision of the EFCB, despite desperate lobbying by Charles Urstadt to preserve the agency's independence. The Authority then experienced significant delays in approvals for even the modest expenditures to install the utilities on the site.

The New York State Fiscal Crisis

Nelson Rockefeller's remarkable building boom was largely funded by "moral obligation bonds," a fiscal instrument devised by the leading bond attorney John Mitchell, before he became prominent as US Attorney General in the Watergate scandal [Bleeker 1981:139]. Most of the new state public authorities, including the BPCA, avoided the need for state-wide referenda on their bond issues by issuing securities which were backed by the "moral obligation" of the State:

> *As one investment broker has said, if one of the state corporations defaulted on debt, it would resemble an elephant dying on the state house steps – the government would have to do something about it or suffer from the stench. [Walsh 1990:204]*

Nelson Rockefeller did not have to worry about the bonds, since he had been appointed to the office of Vice President of the United States after Richard Nixon resigned in August 1974. The BPCA lost its strongest political ally as the fiscal situation in New York state deteriorated. By the end of 1974, there was a definite odor on the steps in Albany. When the Urban Development Corporation defaulted on a bond obligation in January 1975, the market was closed to the State and all its agencies.

Hugh Carey took office as Governor that month. He was the first Democrat elected to that post since 1954. The new administration placed severe borrowing and expenditure restraints upon the government and its independent authorities. The BPCA had to abandon its planned 1976 sale of bonds worth $100 million and the legislature put a cap on BPCA general borrowing at $200 million [NYS L.1976, C.38]. The Housing Revenue Bonds for the first development were put on hold since there was no market. By early 1976, the State was forced to pass legislation preventing future use of "moral obligation" bonds.

State Review of the BPCA's Future

The BPCA tried to keep up the appearance of momentum. They held a "ground breaking" ceremony in September 1974, with Rockefeller's interim replacement, Governor Malcolm Wilson driving the first pile for the residential foundations. In February

1976, State Controller Levitt filed an audit report on the BPCA, calling for a review of the development strategy and greater state oversight. The report noted that principal repayment in the serial bonds would being in 1984, making time a critical factor [NYS Comptroller 1976]. When there was little progress in the construction, the BPCA decided to fund the rest of the residential foundations for Pod III (Gateway Plaza) from their own revenues and held a second ground breaking, with Governor Carey in 1978. Urstadt also negotiated an agreement with New York City where they would install $10 million in infrastructure on the site, but the City could not find the cash.

By the late 1970's construction had still not begun and the Battery Park City site was an embarrassing sea of sand adjacent to the World Trade Center. It became known as "the beach" (Figure 24). The *Wall Street Journal* and *Barron's* both ran articles on the lack of development and questioned whether the bonds could be repaid [Koenig 1977; Klapper 1978].

In January, 1978, the State Assembly Housing Committee voted to conduct a review of the BPCA, chaired by Edward Lehner. He advocated turning the site into an industrial park, while others proposed that it be left as a park. The first public meeting was broken up when the chairman and committee were shouted down by unemployed construction workers who had been encouraged to attend by the BPCA. Charles Urstadt remembers that the agency's relationship with the committee went downhill from there [Urstadt interview 1992].

Hugh Carey was re-elected as governor in November 1978. His administration decided to seize control of several state agencies, including the BPCA, using "recess appointments" to replace directors without approval from the Rebublican-controlled State Senate. Charles Urstadt's term as Chairman expired on December 31, 1978, but he decided to contest the takeover with assistance of the State Senate. He left office a few days later after the Senate Majority Leader withdrew his support.

The Governor's Office transferred control of the BPCA to the Urban Development Corporation in January 1979 by naming William Hasset and Pazel Jackson to its three person Board of Directors. Hasset and Jackson, who were also members of the UDC Board, were named Chairman and Vice-Chairman of BPCA, respectively. Richard A. Kahan was named President of

Figure 24　The Vacant Battery Park City Landfill.
Source: Downtown-Lower Manhattan Association.

both the UDC and BPCA in February 1979. Within weeks, two State Assembly committees reported serious concerns about whether the bonds could be repaid and recommended major changes to the BPCA's role as a public developer. The BPCA's offices were closed and most of its staff were released.

Thirteen years after Nelson Rockefeller announced the project, the BPCA had no buildings under construction and was approaching default on its bonds. Its political support had largely disappeared since the administrations had now changed twice at both levels since the original Rockefeller/Lindsay agreement. It looked like the Battery Park City project was finished.

CHAPTER SIX

Recharging Battery Park City: 1979–82

New York State and the City were still intensely concerned about their financial state in the late 1970's, to the exclusion of concerns about redeveloping Battery Park City. With hindsight, it can be suggested that the BPCA was well positioned to take advantage of an economic recovery, but expectations had been drastically reduced by the fiscal crisis. The New York real estate market had been depressed for most of a decade. Nobody expected it to recover to the levels of the late 1980's boom. Even if they did, the bond principal repayments required in the early 1980's would force the BPCA financial issues before any private sector revenues could begin to flow.

The Downtown-Lower Manhattan Association Intervenes

David Rockefeller and the DLMA watched the decline of the BPCA with dismay. Battery Park City was the only downtown redevelopment project underway in 1978, since Manhattan Landing had never taken off. Charles Urstadt appealed to his old allies for support as he fought for his job in late 1978, and the DLMA wrote the mayor and governor suggesting that the project should be rescued. The DLMA also commissioned a consulting firm to review the Battery Park City plan and report on its financial prospects [Douglass 1995 interview].

The Vollmer Associates report was the first positive review of the project in years and it came at a crucial time. It was sent to the Mayor and Governor in April 1979, only a few weeks after the damaging State Assembly reports and dismantling of the BPCA. The consultants recommended that the State act immediately to install infrastructure, modify the Battery Park City plan and change its approval process to make it more appealing to private investors. Vollmer suggested that the office buildings be moved from the south end of the site to a location adjacent to the World Trade Center in the middle of the site (Figure 25) and that the roads and utilities for the first phase be installed immediately to give confidence to private developers that the project would proceed. They noted that the vacant site and complex approval process made developers reluctant to be the first investor in the project [Vollmer 1979].

On the financial side, the consultants reminded everybody that the Battery Park City site was magnificent, inexpensive and had "tremendous potential value." They calculated that if the agency could develop about half of its office space and one third of its residential units, it could meet its bond obligations. Vollmer calculated that the State would have to provide bridge financing of $30 to $50 million if it took as long as another decade to reach this level of development [Vollmer 1979:8].

The State Work Out Plan

Richard Kahan moved swiftly to deal with the problems at UDC and BPCA:

> Our assignment with the BPCA was to save the bonds. We did not think that we would build. The idea was to bank the land and stop the hemorrhage of cash ... It looked like they would default in 1983 or 1984.
>
> I set up a conference room at the UDC as a work-out room and got about fifty lawyers involved. Most of the group were working on [paying off] the bonds, which we calculated would cost about $130 to 140 million at that point ... There was also a small team in one corner doing a "what if we developed" scenario ... [Kahan interview 1992]

Kahan interviewed three or four urban design firms to assist his work-out team. He had never met Alexander Cooper or Stanton Eckstut, but their young firm came highly recommended by his advisors. They were both former members of the City's Urban

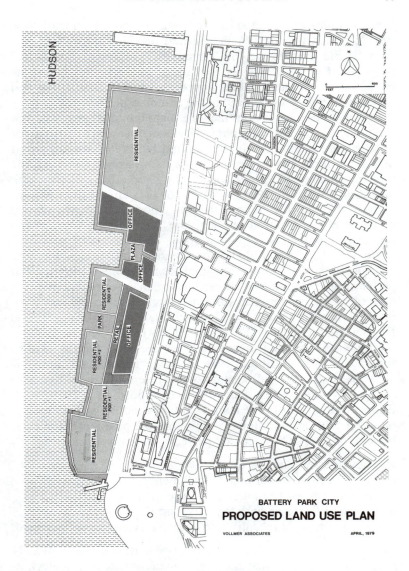

Figure 25 The Downtown-Lower Manhattan Association's Proposed Land Use Plan 1979 (Vollmer Associates).
Source: Downtown-Lower Manhattan Association.

Design Group which acted as a training ground for some of New York's best urban designers [Barnett 1982]. Cooper had just completed a term on the City Planning Commission. Kahan had to get the City to waive its conflict of interest rules before he could interview them. Their approach seemed innovative and practical and they were hired in the summer of 1979.

Cooper and Eckstut examined the planning, market and design problems of the previous plan. The poor market conditions for offices were beginning to turn around by 1979, and the report noted that rents and absorption were rising again. However, the housing market was slow and funding for affordable housing had almost dried up [Cooper 1979:16–17]. Their report recommended that the BPCA move the office node from the South end of the site to a location opposite the World Trade Center, and pursue commercial development first.

Cooper and Eckstut also recommended that the development control strategy of the previous plan be abandoned, and replaced with a simple mapping of streets and urban design guidelines for each block. This approach was much more flexible and less complicated than the Master Development Plan/Master Lease/Special District Zoning Approval [Cooper 1979:91–92].

The work out team discovered that the State would have to spend over $130 million in 1979 to get out of the bonds immediately, but then it would be stuck with the entire ninety-five acre site to sell, which was not an attractive proposition in 1979 [NYS Budget Office 1979]. The team could buy another year to look at building with an additional year's interest payment. However, many tasks had to be executed perfectly in that year:

- a new master plan,
- a new environmental impact statement,
- obtain approval from the legislature,
- get out of the lease with the City, and
- arrange financial incentives to get the private sector interested.

The critical issue for development appeared to be the unwieldy lease with the City. Once again, Kahan defused a difficult technical issue by hiring consultants with good credibility with the local government. The UDC retained the City of New York's two top appraisal firms to get evaluations of the site with the lease in place. One appraisal was zero and the other was negative [Kahan interview 1992]. Kahan then felt ready to approach the City for a new deal.

Negotiating A New Deal with the City

When Edward Koch was elected Mayor of New York in 1977, Battery Park City was not on his priority list:

> *The City was on the edge of bankruptcy. We had lost 600,000 jobs in the last decade and nobody was building ...*
>
> *New York City was down and out. My job was to restore confidence and fiscal stability.*
>
> *Nobody talked about Battery Park City in those days, except Charlie Urstadt. Their bond issue was depleted; only about half of it was left. It was called the "beach" because of the sand dunes on the empty landfill. [Koch interview 1992]*

The bond issues drove the City and State together. The city had finally rehabilitated its credit and had just re-entered the short term bond market in 1979 [Netzer 1990:53]. The suggestion that Battery Park City might default had severe consequences for both parties.

Kahan had trouble getting the City's attention at first, but David Rockefeller helped put the issue before Koch. A high level meeting was arranged at the Mayor's office in September 1979, attended by the Mayor, Deputy Mayors, the Governor's Secretary, Richard Kahan and the State's bond lawyer. Everybody agreed about the emergency and importance of the issue [Kahan and Wagner interviews 1992].

The City's negotiating team was headed by Robert F. Wagner, Jr., the Deputy Mayor for Policy and former Chairman of the City Planning Commission. Wagner was then dealing with bond rating houses, trying to re-establish the City's credit rating. He remembers that the City's negotiating objectives were:

> *1. Relief from our commitment to provide $10 million for infrastructure.*
>
> *2. Some level of control over development, but not necessarily ULURP.*

> 3. *We didn't want the BPCA to take other insti-*
> *tutions from Lower Manhattan. There was*
> *talk of the American Stock Exchange moving*
> *and we wanted to keep the NYSE and the*
> *Federal Reserve Board downtown.*
> 4. *We did not want to set a bad example with tax*
> *incentives which would serve as a precedent*
> *in other more needy areas.*
> 5. *We wanted to get the land back and share in*
> *the profits someday, although nobody thought*
> *it would happen at the time.*
> 6. *To keep Pier A, which the BPCA had threat-*
> *ened to demolish. [Wagner interview 1992]*

The City's team included Wagner, their lawyer, the Budget Director and planner, with the Deputy Mayor for economic development involved in tax issues. Richard Kahan headed the State's team, supported by a lawyer, Alexander Cooper and Stanton Eckstut.

There were two streams to the negotiations: financial issues and design issues. The City wanted out of the $10 million infrastructure commitment, but it did not want to set a precedent by granting the highest (twenty year) level of property tax abatement for a high profile downtown Manhattan site. The tricky issue of a City sale of property to the State was finessed by the appraisals; the UDC could expropriate the lease at a nominal sum.

Surprisingly, the City insisted that all low income housing should be removed from the plan in 1979. Battery Park City would have absorbed New York's entire housing subsidy available, and the City had much higher priority areas in the South Bronx, Brooklyn and Harlem [Wagner interview 1992].

The design issues were no doubt alleviated by the CPC's comfort with Cooper and Eckstut. Wagner remarked that: "Their master plan was very much in keeping with what the CPC was looking for; it was a plan for the 1980's" [Wagner interview 1992]. The City agreed to complete an accelerated review of the office proposals and Master Plan in *fifteen days*. The office development was approved for rezoning and the master plan was given general approval; only the mapping and zoning of the residential neighborhoods would require further review.

The negotiations were intense, but rapid, culminating in a Memorandum of Understanding (MOU) between the Governor, the State, the UDC and the BPCA on November 8, 1979, with these provisions:

1. The state acquired the site through expropriation by the UDC.
2. The approval process was abandoned.
3. Cooper's plan was generally adopted.
4. The city would give tax incentives to office development for 10 years.
5. The city would re-acquire the site when the BPCA's financial obligations were paid off.
6. The state would provide $8 million in loans to guarantee the bonds. [BPCA 1979]

In effect, the city, faced with the project's bankruptcy, gave up its hopes of financial returns, design control and low-income housing in return for the state bailing out the project. Ten years of frustration for the agency were swept away by ten weeks of negotiation.

The MOU was implemented in the June 6, 1980 Settlement Agreement and yet another amendment to the Master Lease. These were approved by a unanimous vote at the CPC and a nine to two vote at the Board of Estimate in June 1980.

A Revised Battery Park City Authority

With the political problems under control, the State felt confident enough to re-establish the BPCA as an independent organization. Richard Kahan hired Barry Light as President and a small staff. They set up offices in temporary trailers installed on the site, to keep overhead down. The staff hired consultants to complete the plan and prepare other reports.

In the meantime, Kahan negotiated interim financial support form the State to pay expenses and cover the bond obligations while the BPCA looked for private investors. The financial situation was serious at the end of 1979 since the first principal payment would be due the next year. The State provided $35.7 million in repayable advances in the five fiscal years from 1979 through 1984 (see Appendix A). Without this bail-out, the BPCA would have defaulted on its bonds.

CHAPTER SEVEN

The 1979 Master Plan

The report prepared by Alexander Cooper and Stanton Eckstut over twelve weeks in the summer of 1979 became the most influential plan in the development of Battery Park City. It guided the rapid development of over half the site in the next eight years and became an icon of post-modern urban design.

A detailed building program was not included in the 1979 Master Plan. The program had to remain essentially unchanged from the 1969 Master Development Plan in order to comply with the conditions of the 1972 bonds, so the new plan included six million square feet of commercial development and between 12,000 and 16,000 residential units in two neighborhoods. It was anticipated that detailed building programs would be developed at the time urban design guidelines were prepared. The Memorandum of Understanding between the City and State was even less specific, since only the six million square feet of office was mentioned.

The most important change to the 1969 land use plan was to move the office node from the southern tip to the center of the site, opposite the World Trade Center. Cooper and Eckstut included a few detailed urban design diagrams for this commercial node, which Richard Kahan wanted to develop immediately.

Physical Design Concept

The primary physical design concept of the 1979 Master Plan was a simple extension of the traditional street and block structure of lower Manhattan. Stanton Eckstut recalls that they prepared for the interview by walking up and down New York streets looking for local precedents: "… we felt that the plan had to be *New York*. This was a risky approach at the time because it was not certain that New York was a good precedent in 1979 …" [Eckstut 1992 interview].

ending the New York street and block fabric and using local precedents may appear to be a conservative approach, but it was a radical design initiative in 1979. For the previous four decades, the redevelopment of cities had been influenced by the techniques of large-scale Modern architecture: superblocks, separation of land uses, elevated streets and building designs which aggressively proclaimed their difference from the historic fabric of the city.

The new plan was based upon eight design principles:

1. Battery Park City should not be a self-contained new-town-in-town, but a part of lower Manhattan.
2. The layout and orientation of Battery Park City should be an extension of lower Manhattan's system of streets and blocks.
3. Battery Park City should offer an active and varied set of waterfront amenities.
4. The design of Battery Park City should take a less idiosyn-cratic, more recognizable, and more understandable form.
5. Circulation at Battery Park City should reemphasize the ground level.
6. Battery Park City should reproduce and improve upon what is best about New York's neighborhoods.
7. Battery Park City's commercial center should become the central focus of the project.
8. Land use and development control should be sufficiently flexible to allow adjustment to future market requirements.
   [Cooper 1979]

These design principles were illustrated by a simple diagram which became the symbol of Battery Park City's new plan (Figure 26). Cooper and Eckstut drew the site and its surround-ings as a 'figure-ground' plan, with the streets and public spaces in white and the private buildings hatched in black, showing the pattern of development but not the specific form of buildings. This style of representation was loaded with symbolic meaning in 1979, since it recalled the presentation of Nolli's 1741 plan of Rome and had recently been featured in the influential book *Collage City* [Rowe and Koetter 1978]. Cooper and Eckstut's plan for Battery Park City was clearly positioned in the vanguard of Post-Modern urban design. The traditional city was now avant-garde.

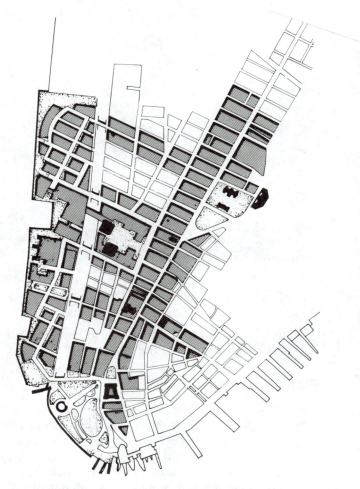

Figure 26 Battery Park City 1979 Figure Ground Plan (Cooper Eckstut).
Source: Cooper 1979.

The 1979 Master Plan focused upon the quality of the public spaces to be created at Battery Park City, rather than attempting to illustrate the design of the buildings. Simple perspective drawings were prepared of the special places in the plan, showing the buildings in outline form and the public spaces in some detail

Figure 27   The South Cove.
Source: Cooper 1979.

(Figure 27). The overall effect was to keep the 1969 land uses but transform the image of the project.

Planning Controls

The 1979 Memorandum of Understanding essentially removed the City of New York from the planning regulation of Battery Park City. The few planning controls in the Memorandum included a height limit of one-half of the World Trade Center for the office development and a density of 15.0 FAR (floor area ratio) for the commercial component. Finally, the amount of office development was limited to six million square feet [BPCA 1979].

   While the Master Plan and planning controls that were developed for Battery Park City in 1979 were fairly general, the detailed design guidelines prepared for each neighborhood were quite specific. Design guidelines were prepared by the BPCA shortly before a commercial developer was to be selected so that the BPCA could maintain flexibility in the detailed execution of its plan. The agency could respond to current market conditions and building form up to the period before a developer had to be selected. Guidelines typically included detailed design for public spaces to be built by the BPCA and block-by-block guidelines which regulated the height, bulk, massing, materials, entrances and ground floor conditions for each building parcel. For example, the design guidelines for five building parcels in the north neighborhood included sixty pages of text and thirty-five illustrative diagrams (Figure 28) [BPCA 1994b].

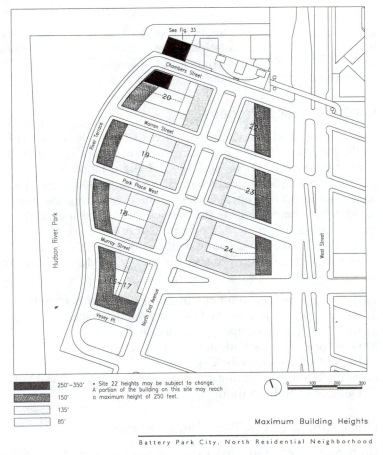

250'–350'
150'
135'
85'

• Site 22 heights may be subject to change. A portion of the building on this site may reach a maximum height of 250 feet.

0 100 200 300

Maximum Building Heights

Battery Park City, North Residential Neighborhood

Figure 28 Building Height Design Guidelines for North Neighbourhood (Ralph Lerner Architect).
Source: Battery Park City Authority 1994b, Figure 22.

Cost Estimates

New cost estimates for infrastructure and public facilities were also developed as part of the 1979 Master Plan [Cooper 1979:95]:

Circulation		$13.7 million
Open space		$31.0 million
Utilities		$ 8.5 million
	Total cost	$53.2 million
		(1979 dollars)

The switch to ordinary streets and parks and the elimination of the megastructure's circulation spine reduced site improvement costs considerably, when compared to the $175 million ($1972) estimated for the earlier plan.

Implementation Process

The 1979 Master Plan was designed to be implemented using well-established techniques such as street mapping and simple zoning classification for building parcels. Mapping the public streets created the building parcels and protected views to the water and important open spaces, without requiring the complicated legal arrangements in the previous lease and special district zoning. A staging plan was prepared to provide for the orderly extension of streets and public facilities (Figure 29).

The implementation process for the 1979 Master Plan contained the following steps:

1. BPCA prepares design guidelines for the neighborhood.
2. BPCA designs and builds roads and public spaces.
3. BPCA selects developers for individual parcels.
4. Developer designs building.
5. Review of design by BPCA.
6. Application for building permits from the City of New York.
7. Developer builds buildings.

Comparison of the Two Master Plans

Both plans were intended to accommodate over five million square feet of office space, and 14,000 to 16,000 residential

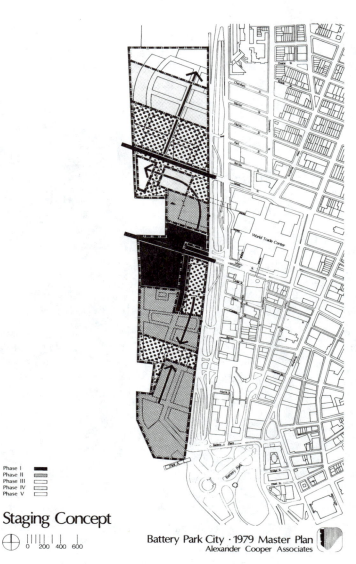

Phase I
Phase II
Phase III
Phase IV
Phase V

Staging Concept

0   200   400   600

Battery Park City · 1979 Master Plan
Alexander Cooper Associates

Figure 29   1979 Staging Plan.
Source: Cooper 1979.

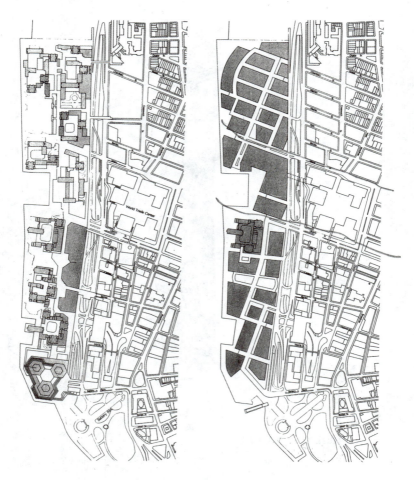

Figure 30   Comparison of the 1969 and 1979 Plans.
Source: Cooper 1979.

units. Most similarities stop there (Figure 30). Philip Johnson
reflected on the rationale behind the 1969 plan:

> *The plan was very much a product of the 1960s. We*
> *were all revolutionaries in those days. It was consid-*
> *ered going backwards to follow the [existing] blocks.*
> *We were like students, creating a tabula rasa ...*
>   *We were so gung-ho about the New City that we*
> *forgot about the old one. [Johnson interview 1992]*

The 1969 megastructure concept reflected a booming economy
and can-do mindset left over from the days of Robert Moses.
Nevertheless, few megastructure plans were ever built, even on a
small scale, except as hospitals, research institutions or government offices. The 1969 megastructure plan was an inflexible,
all-or-nothing concept that required enormous up-front public
investments as a prerequisite for private development. There
were no known example of public/private partnerships as mega-
structures at the time. A circulation system which is even partly
incomplete would be a nuisance and no developer wanted to be
the first on the site when there was any uncertainty about implementation of the spine [Cooper 1979:12]. The Cooper Eckstut
Plan permitted smaller buildings and a smaller development
increment: thirty-six blocks versus seven pods. In addition to a
finer grain of urban fabric, an attribute which is now appreci-
ated, the smaller sites allowed the BPCA to work with many
types of developers rather than the few enormous firms capable
of building a pod.

Streets, blocks and parks were not only cheaper to build than a
spine, but they were also simpler to understand and more public
in nature than grade separated pedestrian decks. The traditional
organizers of private building parcels were also simpler to
implement under existing statutory road building provisions.
The public infrastructure of the megastructure appeared to cost
approximately six times more than the traditional streets and
blocks plan according to the cost estimates prepared for the two
Master Plans (Table 1). Long term maintenance of the complex
structures would also be more expensive and risky, given the
financial constraints and attitude of New York City.

The implementation process of the 1969 Plan contained
approximately fifteen major approvals, versus seven in the

TABLE 1
PLAN IMPLEMENTATION COMPARISON

1969 Master Development Plan	1979 Master Plan
Physical Design Concept:	**Physical Design Concept:**
Megastructure	Extension of Manhattan Grid
Public Circulation Spine	Streets
7 Pods	36 Blocks
Open Space Decks	Public Parks

Planning Controls:

1969	1979
City Ownership	BPCA Ownership
Master Lease	City Repurchase Option
Master Development Plan	Master Plan
Special District Zoning	Urban Design Guidelines

Site Improvement Cost Estimates:

	$1973	$1979 (1)		$1979
Utilities	14.1	25.2	Utilities	8.5
Civic Facilities	41.1	73.6	Civic Facilities	3.0
Streets, Spine	58.3	104.4	Streets	13.7
Foundations	19.2	34.4	Foundations	n/a
Arch & Eng	26.0	46.5	Arch & Eng	incl.
Contingency	15.8	28.3	Contingency	incl.
TOTAL ($million)	$174.5	$312.4	TOTAL ($million)	$53.2

Implementation Process:

1969	1979
1. BPCA designs service spine	1. BPCA prepares design guidelines
2. PARB reviews spine design	2. BPCA designs streets and parks
3. City Plan Comm. Amendments	3. BPCA selects developer(s)
4. Board of Estimate Amendments	4. Developer designs buildings
5. BPCA starts spine construction	5. BPCA reviews designs
6. BPCA selects pod developer	6. BPCA builds streets & parks
7. Developer designs pod platform	7. Developer builds building
8. BPCA reviews pod/spine connect	
9. Developer designs towers	
10. BPCA approves tower design	
11. PARB reviews pod design	
12. CPC amends MDP (if required)	
13. B of E amends MDP (if req.)	
14. Developer builds pod platform	
15. Developer builds first building	

(1) 1973 costs inflated to $1979 using CPI (1973 = 128.4; 1979 = 230.1)
Source: *Economic Report of the President, 1987*

revised Master Plan process. In addition, many of the 1969 approvals were by outside (city) authorities with little incentive for timely action or compromise. The initial implementation process was so cumbersome that only one project (the Lefrak pod) went through it. The cost penalties imposed by delays for minor amendments were so severe that excessive attention was paid to conformance with the rigid zoning requirements and design quality clearly suffered [Cooper 1979, p. 9].

Perhaps the greatest similarity between the two plans was that they were both widely praised by design critics when released. Ada Louise Huxtable applauded the Cooper Eckstut plan: "it has the virtues of simplicity, flexibility, logic and reasonable scale …" [Huxtable 1979]. However, this plan had lasting appeal beyond the architectural critics. The flood of praise continued as the project gained momentum. By the end of the decade, the master plan had become an icon of urban design in the 1980's [Dixon 1993; Time 1990]. More important to the BPCA and the people of New York, the plan facilitated immediate development of the site.

CHAPTER EIGHT

Building Battery Park City

The BPCA was rescued in the nick of time. It might have gone bankrupt by defaulting on its bonds in the next year. Once restructured, however, the project revived quickly. Over half the project started construction in the next five years.

Gateway Plaza

The first buildings at Battery Park City were the ill-fated Pod III which Lefrak and Fisher had been attempting to develop for almost eight years. The BPCA and the City still had some concerns about the plain design of the complex, which was targeted at middle income renters. Cooper and Eckstut worked with Lefrak's architects to move the upper level retail facilities down to grade, and fit the buildings into the streets, but it was still a large, boxy concrete pod. However, it was assumed that it was important to have construction going on the site when the BPCA sought bids for the commercial parcels [Burden interview 1992]. The issue became moot when the financing arrived.

The long awaited FHA mortgage insurance was finally granted in May 1980, and the BPCA obtained the highest rating (AAA) from Standard & Poors for its Housing Revenue Bonds. The authority was then able to sell $115,920,000 worth of bonds in one day. Construction started in June 1980. The 1712 apartments at Gateway Plaza were occupied in June 1982.

Battery Park City's first residents had arrived a little over sixteen years after Nelson Rockefeller's press conference.

The World Financial Center

An earlier plan to move the American Stock Exchange to the site fell apart by October 1980, so the office parcels in the new

Master Plan were the key to the long term solvency of the
BPCA. Richard Kahan wanted to obtain a good return on these
sites, but he had to change the attitude of the property market:

> The marketplace psychology about Battery Park
> City was awful. Our own real estate consultants,
> Landauer, said that it couldn't be done because of
> Westway and the "sand dune" had been out there too
> long. The BPCA had no credibility because it kept
> holding ground-breaking ceremonies, and nothing
> was built after twelve years.
>   We reversed the psychology through the design.
> The Esplanade was a tangible thing which we did at
> the highest quality.
>   After that it was easier to get interest in the site. I
> wanted to create a frenzy in the market, so I invited
> the big developers in one at a time to see the new
> plans. [Kahan interview 1992]

Kahan had Cooper Eckstut Associates prepare detailed planning
criteria and urban design guidelines for the commercial site in a
200 page report. These guidelines were the basis for accurate
cost estimates for the BPCA's infrastructure investment. They
were also used as a basis for evaluating developer submissions
for the site [Cooper interview 1986].

The authority invited approximately thirty developers to
make proposals for office developments in July, 1980. They
received twelve submissions. Olympia & York Developments
of Toronto was designated to undertake the entire office project
in September, 1980. The designation came as something of a surprise as O & Y were not well known in New York at the time,
despite having acquired the office holdings of the Uris organization in 1976.

O & Y demonstrated a unique understanding of the BPCA's
financial situation:

> While other contenders had come to Kahan with
> grandiose architectural visions for the site, Paul
> Reichmann came with a single, folded, blue sheet of
> paper in his pocket. The sheet contained not an archi-
> tectural outline but a series of numbers. The numbers
> were the repayment schedule on the $200 million of

*bonds that the authority had floated some years before.
"If I were to guarantee these bond repayments," asked
Reichmann, "would I be on the right track?"*

*Reichmann had gone straight to the heart of the
officials' most pressing problem: the threat of default
on the bonds.*

*While other developers were still treating the
project as a normal development, Paul Reichmann
had seen that the required solution was not architectural but financial. He offered an ironclad set of
guarantees. If there was a delay in construction,
letters of credit ensured that O & Y would still pay
the $50 million in ground rent and taxes it would owe
if the buildings were finished. He also undertook to
build the project much faster than any of the other
contestants, in five years. [Foster 1986:44–45]*

In addition to fitting the agency's needs, the O & Y offer of rent
and Payments In Lieu Of Taxes (PILOT) had the highest net
present value to the BPCA.

Most developers brought a set of fancy drawings and a condi-
tional financial offer to the agency. In addition to its innovative
financial structure, O & Y also flouted tradition by not bringing a
fixed design to the negotiating table. Instead, they invited three
leading architectural firms (Kohn Pederson Fox; Mitchell
Giurgola and Cesar Pelli) to participate in a limited design competition, based upon the BPCA design guidelines. The proposal
of Cesar Pelli was selected in May 1981. Pelli caught the spirit
of the new plan by rendering his scheme in the style of Hugh
Ferris, the illustrator of the 1920's-era skyscrapers (Figure 31).
The design was hailed as the "next Rockefeller Center" by *The
New York Times*' critic Ada Louise Huxtable [Huxtable 1981].

While O & Y's financial and design strategy were impressive,
their real achievement was in repositioning Battery Park City as a
head office location for investment firms. They named the office
complex the "World Financial Center." O & Y offered a novel
leasing deal, where they bought the older buildings of tenants
who needed a capital gain, and leased them space at the WFC.
They attracted the head offices of American Express, Merrill
Lynch, Dow Jones and Oppenheimer, leasing almost six million
square feet of space between 1981 and 1985, despite a recession.

Figure 31   World Financial Centre Rendering (Cesar Pelli).
Source: Battery Park City Authority.

The O & Y ground lease was signed in September 1981 and construction on the entire site began three months later, thanks to the accelerated planning process in the new agreement with the City. The first tenants moved in during the fall of 1985.

The revenue from the O & Y ground leases began in 1981 and escalated to $50 million by 1993 [BPCA 1993]. This lease alone more than covered the annual cost of the BPCA's 1972 bond obligations, without any revenue from the 14,000 apartment units permitted on the site. The financial future of the agency was assured by the first development project following its revival.

Public Spaces and Facilities

The new plan for Battery Park City placed a considerable emphasis on the role of public space in shaping the image of the project to the rest of the city and to potential private investors. The BPCA built most of the public spaces itself. It completed the spaces in advance of private development in order to increase the value of the adjacent sites.

The Cooper Eckstut plan described a general program for the major public spaces, but detailed designs would be required to allow the BPCA to build the public realm. One of Richard Kahan's first appointments was Amanda Burden as Vice President of Architecture and Urban Design, responsible for design review and development of the public spaces. Both Burden and Stanton Eckstut credit Kahan for being determined to produce the highest quality public spaces at an early date, during a period when the agency was close to bankruptcy.

The first project was the Esplanade in front of Gateway Plaza. Eckstut was concerned about the image created by those first buildings and worked with Hanna Olin on the Esplanade design:

> *I wanted to use the traditional New York City parks materials: the hexagonal pavers, benches, railings, lights and granite. The Parks department did not accept the design at first; they were not using the traditional materials then. We did models of the proposals and photographed them against the actual Hudson River view. [Eckstut interview 1992]*

Amanda Burden noted that their detailed work on the multiple uses for public spaces was influenced by the advice of William H. Whyte. He had spent over a decade observing how New Yorkers use streets and small urban spaces [Whyte 1989]. However, there were also strong financial reasons for the design strategy:

> *A lot of the decisions were influenced by marketing. We were building a new town in an unproven area, and we wanted to get people to go there. Stan [Eckstut] wanted it to be familiar to New Yorkers.*
>
> *We built models and a mock-up on the site, with the sand blowing around. The railing design was*

Figure 32   Battery Park City Esplanade (Cooper Eckstut and Hanna Olin).
Source: Battery Park City Authority.

> *modified because we found that it blocked your view*
> *as you sat on the benches. When people were shown*
> *the model photographs, they often said "I've been*
> *there ..." [Burden interview 1992]*

The first phase of the Esplanade opened in June 1983 and was an immediate critical and popular success (Figure 32). New Yorkers strolled the walkway and enjoyed the view, despite the difficulty in reaching a site isolated by construction and the West Side highway.

The BPCA was soon launched into an extensive program of public space design for Rector Place and the World Financial Center. A Public Art Advisory Committee was set up to commission artists to work with the architects designing the public spaces. The public art program started tentatively at the WFC and Rector Park and entered into a full scale collaboration between artist Mary Miss and Stanton Eckstut for the South Cove, which opened in 1988. The BPCA's approach to public art has been praised for its process and its results [Larson 1985; Johnson 1990].

The Battery Park City Authority attempted to meet its public mandate by developing extraordinary public spaces and institutions to invite all people onto the site [Frucher interview 1992]. The first of the new public facilities was the Winter Garden in the World Financial Center, designed by Cesar Pelli. The 120 foot high room is home to sixteen palm trees and frequent public events throughout the year [Goldberger 1988]. With its grand entrance staircase and soaring glass vault, the Winter Garden is a public space on the scale of the concourse at Grand Central Station. It could easily have descended into the private world of shopping malls and corporate atria, the modern precedent for such spaces, but the combination of the movable tables and chairs, pedestrians lounging on the steps, and the dramatic view into the bay make it a successful public space.

The next public institution to be added to the site was a new home for Stuyvesant High School, one of New York's premier public schools. The new school and swimming pool is built on a 1.3 acre site donated by the BPCA at the north end of the site. Stuyvesant High was built by the BPCA in order to save time and money compared to the City's normal construction process. The school opened in 1992 after a controversy about access over the busy West Side highway. The BPCA eventually agreed to share the $1.5 million cost of a pedestrian bridge at the Chambers Street intersection.

The next public facility was the Holocaust Museum, a proposal which moved from site to site at Battery Park City after 1986. This Jewish cultural center and memorial was eventually given a waterfront site in the Battery Place neighborhood but its construction stalled in the recession in the early 1990's.

The careful attention to detail and design quality in public spaces worked. By 1986, with only a fraction of the buildings completed, Battery Park City was being hailed as "The Next Great Place" [Wiseman 1986]. As the rest of the parks and walkways were completed, other observers heaped praise on the project [Gill 1990; Starr 1993].

Rector Place

The second phase of residential development was Rector Place, with 2200 units on ten parcels south of Gateway Plaza. The BPCA had already obtained the zoning for the neighborhood and mapped the streets after the 1980 agreement with the City. The agency then designed and built Rector Park and the streets prior to completion of the private buildings.

The BPCA retained Cooper Eckstut to prepare detailed urban design guidelines for each parcel in the neighborhood. These guidelines were the basis for the proposal call to developers advertised in April 1981. Twenty-seven developers responded, and six were selected to build in the neighborhood. Stanton Eckstut believes that the BPCA got more responses and higher bids because they created certainty for the developers.

The Battery Park City Authority did the planning, got the approvals and built the infrastructure. All the developer had to do was go for a building permit. This situation was almost unheard of in New York City.

The developer's architect could work faster because the context and basic massing were set; some of the teams were able to submit for a permit within three months. This process saved time and created value for the developer, which was reflected in the responses to the proposal calls.

The six developers were selected in August 1981 and most entered into the BPCA's design review process, according to the process specified in the proposal call and ground lease. The developer's architect submitted their design drawings to the BPCA staff, who had ten working days to turn around each submission, or it was automatically approved. The BPCA staff checked the drawings for adherence to the design guidelines and negotiated changes where necessary.

The financial approvals for the six projects at Rector Place moved more slowly. The developers were selected just before the 1982 recession and delayed the lease negotiations in order to avoid committing their own cash to projects when the banks were not lending. When the Chairman and President of the BPCA resigned at the end of 1983, there were further delays while the developers slowed negotiations again, waiting for the new team. The leases were finally signed and construction began in early 1984.

The Rector Place buildings have been completed and occupied since 1986, so it has been possible to examine the results of the plan. The guidelines were generally praised for creating variety on a number of different parcels, although some observers later criticized the agency's attempts to recreate the image of older

New York neighborhoods on a brand new site (Russell 1994; Boyer 1988). Perhaps the most serious criticism is that the developers only produced small apartments which were unsuitable for families [Plunz 1990] and limited the market for a home at Battery Park City. A number of smaller issues, like the location and treatment of arcades and service driveways were criticized and recommended for alteration in future phases [Fisher 1988].

Perhaps the best comparison is to the Gateway Plaza, the project completed under the old development process, only a few years before. The Rector Place neighborhood is clearly more successful as a public place and as a residential neighborhood.

Battery Place

The BPCA followed up the success of Rector Place by preparing guidelines and issuing a proposal call for the Battery Place residential area at the south end of the site. The agency was able to select developers for Parcels 4, 10 and 11 before the 1987 stock market crash slowed residential real estate development. The three developers built their projects but the other six blocks remain vacant. The recession hit the three projects hard and condominium sales were slow. One developer went bankrupt before its building sold out and many units were rented by their owners.

Once again, the BPCA built the streets and public spaces for the neighborhood in advance, this time with mixed results. The Esplanade and South Cove, a collaboration between Eckstut and the artist Mary Miss opened in July 1988 and is generally considered to be a fine public place [Howett 1989]. On the other hand, the plans for the South Garden became embroiled in a political and design controversy. The South Garden was a collaboration between the artist Jennifer Bartlett and Alexander Cooper, commissioned in 1985. The artist's vision of a series of twenty-four garden rooms surrounded by high hedges was attacked by community groups who wanted an active park. Many landscape and garden designers also questioned the scheme. The Authority supported the design team for six years, perhaps as a result of their previous success with artist/architect collaborations, but eventually Governor Cuomo canceled the project in October 1991 [McHugh 1991].

The BPCA started afresh, selecting noted urban designers
Machado and Silvetti and landscape architect Laurie Olin, who
worked on the original esplanade design. The new team worked
with the community from the beginning and produced a plan that
won popular and critical support. In a sentimental touch, the park
was named after the late Robert Wagner, Jr., the popular New
York civil servant who negotiated the new plan for Battery Park
City in 1979.

The North Neighborhood

Development of the final neighborhood, at the north end of the
site, was delayed by the slump in the real estate market that
began in 1989. There was significant community input into the
planning of the neighborhood, because the zoning needed to
be approved by Manhattan Community Board No. 1 under the
Uniform Land Use Review Process (ULURP). By 1987, there
were several thousand people living at Battery Park City, and the
residents of the adjacent TriBeCa and West Village neighborhoods began to take an active interest in the planning of the area.

The residents' principal demand was an increase in the amount
of space for active recreation and children's play. Following CB
No. 1's rejection of the application by a vote of two to thirty-two
on November 18, 1986, the BPCA negotiated a new program for
the North Park that included significant active recreation facilities and a permanent recreation staff. The revised plan was
approved by the City Planning Commission in early 1987 [NY
CPC January 28, 1987: Cal.43].

The BPCA retained the Cambridge firm of Carr Lynch Hack
Sandell to design the North Park. Gary Hack was then embroiled
in another complex controversy, designing the Hudson River
Waterfront with intense public participation. Hack suggested
that the BPCA fund a landscape architect to work with the community group in the design process. The resulting design of
North Park was a collaboration between the community and the
Authority, which met with enthusiastic participation of the
children of the area when it opened in June 1992 (Figure 33).

Alexander Cooper prepared design guidelines for the area in
1987, which were used to build the streets and lay out the blocks.

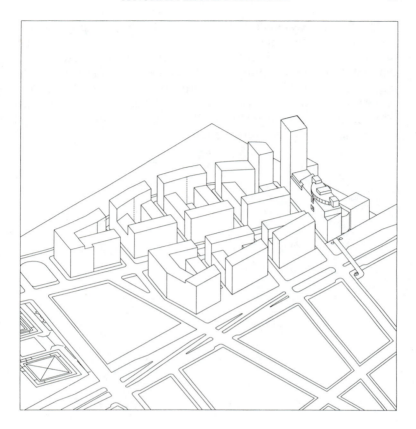

Axonometric Looking North−West
of the North Residential Neighborhood

Battery Park City, North Residential Neighborhood

Figure 33   North Neighbourhood Perspective (Ralph Lerner Architect).
Source: Battery Park City Authority.

All of the building parcels were delayed by the late 1980's real
estate collapse. By the time the market struggled back to its feet
in the mid-1990's, the BPCA had retained new urban design consultants to take a fresh look at the site. The agency retained

Ralph Lerner Architects and James S. Polshek to prepare new guidelines which required a somewhat less historicist approach to the design of the buildings. The new guidelines anticipated that 3300 to 4000 dwelling units could be accommodated on the eight residential blocks in the north neighborhood. The BPCA released three of these blocks in a RFP in mid-1994. Three rental housing developers were selected, but the continuing poor real estate market delayed construction.

CHAPTER NINE

Issues for the 21st Century

Over the next decade, the Battery Park City Authority must make the transition from its role as a public developer of a prime property to a wealthy landowner. While development of the remaining sites is by no means a simple task, more of the Authority's effort is likely to be absorbed in financial and ownership issues like its corporate financial structure, affordable housing, the changing relationship with the City and the residents, and site management.

Corporate Structure

The BPCA has several tasks to accomplish in the new century:

- develop the remainder of the vacant parcels
- construct the remaining public spaces
- act as landlord for the developed parcels
- act as a bank for City housing and financial purposes
- operate the public spaces of the site as a public agency

It is unlikely that this organization can execute all of these different tasks as effectively as they had developed the site since 1979. The Authority achieved a level of excellence in redevelopment implementation by establishing room to operate as an independent, focused organization. The BPCA's independence will be further reduced by legal and political agreements, if the trends of the early 1990's continue.

The Authority took some steps to deal with its split objectives. The Battery Park City Parks Corporation (BPCPC) was set up in 1989 to operate and maintain the public parks. The City of New York could not afford to take on the responsibility at the time of the 1979 negotiations and its financial position was perhaps worse two decades later. The City effectively abandoned the

maintenance of many other parks to the care of adjacent landown-
ers by severely cutting its parks staff and budget. The BPC Parks
Corporation operates and maintains the parks at a high standard,
and insulates the BPCA from the day-to-day problems of operating the site [Huxley interview 1992]. Unlike the business partnerships that maintain many of the downtown streets and parks, the
BPCA tries to preserve a public face by hiring New York City
park rangers to patrol its spaces, rather than privately uniformed
guards. This structure seems like it may keep a responsive public
role in operating the spaces, as an alternative to abandoning them
to neglect by the NYC Parks Department.

The conflict between the roles of the developer, landlord and
bank may require some further organizational adjustments. As
the schools and public realm are completed it will be possible to
wind down the agency's construction function. Similarly, when
the design controls are approved for the remaining parcels, it
may be tempting for the State to sell the remaining sites, or pri-
vatize the development function of the corporation [Pitruzello
1995; Emil and Serpico 1992 interviews].

The landlord and bank issues might require another major
accommodation with the City of New York, which still holds a
right to re-acquire the property at the end of the century, if all the
outstanding financial obligations are repaid. Given the parlous
state of the City's finances, this scenario seems unlikely.

The Battery Park City Authority will probably continue to
balance between its obligations as a public agency and its opportunities as a landlord as it enters the twenty-first century. The dif-
ficulties will arise in trying to implement both objectives at its
current standard of excellence.

Affordable Housing

The BPCA's financial fortunes changed rapidly after the 1979
crisis. While Governor Carey's administration saw the project as
a fiduciary responsibility, when Mario Cuomo took office as
Governor in 1983, he wanted the project to have a rationale
above and beyond economics. He asked his new BPCA president, Sandy Frucher, to "give the project a soul" [Frucher interview 1992]. By this time, the agency's financial future had been

secured by the World Financial Center and it looked like it would
be producing cash by the mid-1990's.

Frucher proposed to the Governor that the BPCA borrow
against this future revenue stream to fund affordable housing, an
original objective of the project which had been dropped three
times during the efforts to get development going. The Governor
and the Mayor supported the idea, but the location issue came up
again, just as it had in John Lindsay and Nelson Rockefeller's
day: should the authority build a modest amount of affordable
housing on site, or use the revenues from developing this valuable property to fund a large housing program where it was
needed most?

Frucher met with the leaders of the Black and Hispanic com-
munities to discuss the allocation issue:

> *I had a simple question: "Would you like the money
> spent in your neighborhood or this neighborhood?"
> They all said that they wanted the affordable housing
> built in the existing minority neighborhoods.*
>
> *Some people argue that there is a moral obligation
> to include affordable housing on the site, but every
> community does not need to be economically inte-
> grated. [Frucher interview 1992]*

Mayor Ed Koch had the same opinion, and the issue was
resolved just as John Lindsay suggested in 1967: market development at Battery Park City subsidized affordable housing in the
South Bronx and Harlem.

The first announcements were for $400 million to be provided
to the City's Housing New York program. The City wanted
control of the money, so the Housing New York Corporation
(HNYC) was established to issue bonds against the Authority's
future revenues [Siroka interview 1992]. The first bond issue of
$218 million netted approximately $143 million for the City's
use [HNYC 1987].

The first projects of the affordable housing initiative were
completed in 1992. The New York City Housing Development
Corporation (HDC) rehabilitated 1557 apartments and community facilities in vacant City-owned buildings in two sites.
Fourteen abandoned buildings were renovated to create 893 units

in the South Bronx by the Crenulated Company, a local not-for-profit corporation. A further forty vacant buildings and 664 units were renewed in Central Harlem in Manhattan by the New York City Housing Authority. All of the units were occupied by persons and families whose incomes were less than the NYC area median [BPCA 1993:I–24] (Figure 34). This scattered approach turned out to be slow and expensive, so HDC switched to a "vacant cluster" program which sold empty buildings to non-profit developers in smaller groups. Another 2128 units were rescued in the South Bronx under this program. HDC committed $312 million to those programs through fiscal year 1992, with other revenues covering the shortfall beyond the bonds backed by the BPCA [NYC HPD 1991:2].

By late 1985, Battery Park City was widely regarded as a financial success, and the Mayor and the Governor were able to announce that another $600 million would be provided for the City's use. Their December, 1989 agreement had a small loophole which also allowed the funds to go to the general fund of the City to maintain existing City services [BPCA 1989:11].

Figure 34   Harlem Housing Rehabilitated with Battery Park City Funds. *Source*: New York City Housing Development Corporation.

New York City's finances deteriorated rapidly as the city slid into a recession in the late 1980's, and newly elected Mayor David Dinkins was forced to adopt some desperate remedies to reduce the budget deficit. Affordable housing initiatives were put on hold, and BPCA revenues were diverted into the City's general fund. The BPCA issued $222.6 million in Revenue Bonds in 1990 which provided $150 million to the City budget [BPCA 1990b]. Financial analysts condemned the move as a return to the practices which had led the City close to bankruptcy in the 1970's. The 1990 bonds capitalized a long term future revenue stream from the BPCA's payments in lieu of taxes and rent to make a 'one-shot' reduction in the City's operating deficit [Sagalyn 1992].

As the City's financial situation worsened, it began to regard Battery Park City as a cash cow which it could milk to supplement its budget. The BPCA was dismayed to see its hard-earned revenue disappear with no tangible results. The City wanted to divert the maximum revenue to its deficit, while the agency wanted to finish its infrastructure program and build affordable housing. The result was a series of difficult negotiations over the BPCA's spending plans. The simple relationship of 1979 was transformed by a complex series of financial agreements between the two parties as they wrestled for control over the cash and bonding capacity generated by the project.

The off-site housing programs were effectively suspended by the 1990 City budget cutbacks. After several years of negotiations, the City and the Authority agreed that the BPCA should provide an additional $198 million for "preservation, rehabilitation and construction of affordable housing" over a five year period beginning in 1994 [BPCA 1994a:16]. It was not clear whether the language in this agreement was strong enough to bind the new administration at City Hall and Albany, both of which placed a lower priority on affordable housing than Mayor Dinkins and Governor Cuomo.

The collapse of the luxury condominium market forced the BPCA to reconsider its target market for the project. With fewer high income young professionals from the financial district willing to purchase the small, expensive apartments in Battery Place, the agency began to consider how to broaden its market to include middle income families. They commissioned several leading housing designers, including Joan Goody, to make suggestions on how apartment buildings on the site could be made more affordable and suitable for families with children. Loft conversions in nearby TriBeCa in the early 1990's gave some hope that the agency might attract this group, but the lack of community services was a substantial concern. The BPCA secured approvals and funding to build a new elementary and middle school in the north neighborhood in 1995, which should significantly increase the appeal of the site to families with children. The first three projects for the north neighborhood were proposed to be funded from the eighty percent market/twenty percent assisted housing rental program, while the BPCA itself intended to build an affordable rental building over the elementary school [BPCA 1994a].

In effect, the BPCA was leveraging its expertise in developing community infrastructure – parks and schools – to create a new market for its housing sites.

Dealing with the City and Residents

Mayor Ed Koch regarded Battery Park City as an economic issue, rather than a political issue when he took office in 1978:

> *There were not many people down there at the time. Community Board No. 1 was not heavily involved. They were a business-oriented Board then; they would have loved the project. [Koch interview 1992]*

For many years he was right, and the Authority had the political freedom to develop its property. As more residents arrived, the balance of power on the Community Board shifted, and local politicians and the residents of Battery Park City and adjacent areas gained input into the development of the remainder of the site, starting with the North Park and South Garden issues. They also lobbied for community facilities, especially for the unexpected number of children squeezed into the small apartments. This situation is a healthy trend since it demonstrates that Battery Park City is becoming a part of the New York local politics.

A less comforting aspect of this trend is the residents' proprietary attitude towards the site. The parks are maintained by the Battery Park City Parks Corporation, which is partially funded by fees assessed against each building on the site. Some residents objected to paying for maintenance of a public park and, as apartment values dropped in the early 1990's, one condominium sued the BPCA to have the fees reduced. Another residents' association worried about the new design of Wagner Park, since it included the long-delayed connection of the waterfront esplanade to Battery Park at the tip of Manhattan, which was, of course, exactly the reason for planning a continuous waterfront walkway: "that certainly looks like a written invitation for people to go from Battery Park to the esplanade ... I'm not saying that we should put a moat around Battery Park City ..." [Downtown Express 1994:4].

The BPCA gently resisted these exclusionary aspects of community participation, keeping its eye on the wider benefits of public access to the site.

The agency got involved in plans to improve public access on a wider scale during the early 1990's. The Downtown Lower Manhattan Association recognized that the 1966 Lower Manhattan Plan was out of date. They lobbied the Dinkins administration to update the plan, but while the City had planning staff, they had no funds to undertake the project. The DLMA raised money from the private sector and BPCA to pay for background studies and technical support for a new land use plan [NY CPC 1993a]. It was released in the last months of David Dinkin's term as mayor, but the new Giuliani administration did not adopt the plan. They preferred to focus on regulatory changes to facilitate development [NYC Lower Manhattan Task Force 1994]. The BPCA tried another approach, engaging architect Steven Peterson to expand the land use proposals as the *Lower Manhattan Urban Design Plan* (Figure 35), which won another award for its sweeping redesign of the downtown area [Progressive Architecture 1995]. The seeds of this urban design scheme also fell on stony ground at a City Hall focused on fiscal issues. The time for bold redevelopment proposals for Lower Manhattan may have passed.

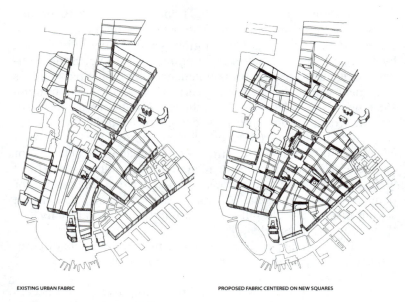

EXISTING URBAN FABRIC   PROPOSED FABRIC CENTERED ON NEW SQUARES

Figure 35   Battery Park City Authority's Lower Manhattan Urban Design Plan 1994 (Steven Peterson Architect).
Source: Battery Park City Authority.

Market Issues

The BPCA recovered from the early 1980's recession quite well. Most of New York City's job losses from that period had been related to manufacturing, while the mid-1980's economic expansion was led by the finance, insurance and real estate sectors, which are traditional consumers of office space. The BPCA took advantage of this situation by rapidly leasing most of its office sites and one-third of its residential sites. However, the recession of the early 1990's may prove to be a different story, since a substantial decline in finance and service sector employment took place in both New York City as a whole and Manhattan [New York Department of City Planning 1994:Ch.2].

The BPCA took advantage of the one benefit of the early 1990's recession – lower interest rates – by re-financing its bonds. The agency simplified the complicated debt structure created by its five previous bond issues by consolidating them in a massive re-financing at the end of 1993. These bonds were issued at a fifteen year low point in interest rates, which reduced the BPCA's debt service by $13 million annually [BPCA 1994a].

The financial future of the agency is based upon assumptions that the remainder of the site can be developed according to the Master Plan. In 1995, another sixteen sites were available for approximately 6000 residential units, and only two sites were available for mixed use, which could include more office space north of the WFC. Thus, any additional long term value created by the project will depend upon the recovery of the residential housing market in New York City.

Battery Park City is well positioned to exploit a residential market recovery, since most of its sites are zoned and ready for development. A location which was considered to have no value 15 years earlier became some of the most lucrative property in the country. The Authority's proven record at putting developers in place to exploit market trends may serve it well.

The office market may be a more difficult issue. While the WFC has established the site as a prime office location, the downtown Manhattan market collapsed in the early 1990's as an over-supply of new space coincided with declining demand. The office vacancy rate soared to nineteen percent in 1992 [Cushman & Wakefield 1995]. Proposals to expand the World Financial Center to the north were shelved and the BPCA searched for a public office tenant for Site 15, adjacent to the water's edge. After little success courting a UN agency, they landed the New York Mercantile Exchange, which signed a lease for the parcel in 1995. The agency will likely hold on to the option of producing one more commercial office building, but the site would probably be suitable for housing. It may end up being the last parcel developed at Battery Park City.

CHAPTER TEN

Why Battery Park City Matters

Battery Park City is a "good news story" in a city that sorely needs one. It would be worth examining, even if it was simply the most important waterfront project in North America's largest city. As urban renewal projects go, it appeared to be doomed to failure at the beginning. In the early 1980's, Ada Louise Huxtable noted that "you could call the story of Battery Park City a cliffhanger, if it were possible to hang onto a cliff for so many years" [1981].

One of the important lessons of the BPCA saga was that it will take decades to implement a big redevelopment project. Battery Park City is still only fifty percent complete thirty years after Nelson Rockefeller's announcement, and it has moved fairly quickly compared to other major waterfront projects [Gordon 1996]. Implementation ebbs and flows with the political and economic cycles, and all aspects of a redevelopment agency's activities must be structured on the assumption that it is engaged in a long-term endeavor, not a "one-shot" real estate project. Planning for this type of activity needs an underlying framework which is robust, and a process which allows quick reaction and minor adjustments to accommodate the fleeting opportunities which appear over the years.

Political Management

The early years of Battery Park City are almost a textbook example of how to bungle the political start-up of a redevelopment project. In a "strong mayor" city like New York, good relations with the political administration at City Hall are a high priority for a redevelopment authority. Nelson Rockefeller and John Lindsay shared the same patrician background, party affiliations, and activist bent, but unfortunately New York City wasn't

99

big enough to contain their ambitions. They competed over everything from waterfront redevelopment to the U.S. presidential nomination. Unilateral action by an upper level of government is a redevelopment tactic that rarely works, and the Governor's 1966 press conference created both resentment and a resistance along every step of the start-up process.

A waterfront redevelopment agency must manage its relationship with the local government, which typically has ownership or control over most utilities, street access, education, community services, police and fire protection. An intransigent municipal government can delay and frustrate implementation, even if the agency owns its own land and has absolute planning authority. The BPCA had neither ownership nor authority, so the city planners could inflict the "death of a thousand cuts" by red tape and delay. Even though the Governor and Mayor eventually signed an agreement in 1969, a redevelopment project with multiple sites requires a more cooperative local approvals strategy than the typical private real-estate deal, since the agency must return to the well repeatedly over the years, rather than simply focusing all its political resources on a single vote.

It took two complete changes of regime in the offices of the governor and mayor to erase the bad relationship between the City and State. When the UDC decided to try to rescue the BPCA in 1979, it went straight to Mayor Koch to negotiate completely new legal and planning foundations for the project. Richard Kahan used consultants with good local reputations to co-opt the technical staff. He hired the city's usual assessors to value the site, while Cooper and Eckstut (former City staff) produced a scheme which was enthusiastically endorsed by the planners and City Planning Commission.

The re-constituted BPCA demonstrated more good political strategy by developing and promoting first-rate public places on the site. These not only improved the value of the adjacent property, but they proved to be political assets as well. The agency actively sought opportunities to link private development with public benefits like the Holocaust Museum and Stuyvesant High School. It also preferred benefits, such as parks, which served the wider community since these tangible benefits were political assets for its sponsoring government and the City.

The affordable housing controversy at Battery Park City was more a political problem than a financial or planning difficulty. There was an ironic twist to the situation, since the usual roles in the drama seemed often to be reversed. Instead of the local government forcing affordable housing on a greedy and recalcitrant developer, the City of New York repeatedly requested that money be spent elsewhere, on other things. The BPCA initially wanted to build a mixed income project, but Mayors Lindsay and Koch wanted any precious affordable housing funds spent in neighborhoods with the greatest need, like Harlem, Brooklyn and the South Bronx. Mayor Dinkins went further, diverting BPCA funds to the City's deficit. These proposals, while economically efficient, did not address the symbolic politics of a public agency building a high profile project.

Battery Park City was just too prominent a target. The high quality offices and expensive housing could be dismissed as a playground for fat-cat bankers and homes for yuppies. Some critics had a fine time with the imagery, decrying public investment in a neighborhood for the rich, while ignoring the fine public spaces and off-site affordable housing funding, or dismissing them as mere palliatives [Boyer 1994, 1988; Russell 1994; Fainstein 1994]. The BPCA got little credit for pledging even $1 billion towards affordable housing. If anything its critics grew even harsher, hinting at conspiracies to keep the poor and the homeless off the site to improve property values for rich people. The critics seemed to demand a symbolic victory – fewer affordable housing units but in a mixed-income neighborhood.

The BPCA mishandled the symbolic politics of this issue, since their efficient proposals appeared to be elitist. The City and agency were simply pursuing niche strategies – maximizing revenue on the waterfront and directing subsidies and community services to needy neighborhoods. The BPCA's strategy proved defective when it turned out that there were not enough high-income residents to fill the 14,000 apartments planned for the site. The agency is now building community services and pursuing middle- and low-income tenants for the North Neighborhood. The value of diversity is now clear, and the agency might have been able to redistribute much of the surplus revenue from the commercial offices while also building a mixed income neighborhood.

Long Term Financial Management

In contrast to the early political battles, the financial start-up of Battery Park City went quite smoothly. The agency negotiated a small loan from local banks and $5.1 million in State appropriations. However, the BPCA actually obtained most of its working capital from the municipal bond market, with its $200 million issue in 1972. This does not imply that the start-up grants were not needed, or that the BPCA was not subsidized, since the bonds had lower interest costs as a result of their tax-exempt status and the moral obligation of the state. However, the BPCA did minimize the *cash* cost to its sponsoring government, which is not an insignificant achievement in these times of severe public sector fiscal constraint.

The reserves in the 1972 bond issue were not large enough to ride out the severe 1975 to 1980 New York fiscal crisis, illustrating the need for the financial structure of a redevelopment project to assume that the build-out period will include years with no new private investment due to the cycles in the real estate market. State bridge financing was needed to carry the project from 1980 to 1986, but the state cash subsidies were later repaid with interest, a rare event in the history of redevelopment projects, which are usually regarded as black holes that governments shovel cash into.

The BPCA financial strategy is a good example of a match between long-term funding (bonds), for long term improvements (infrastructure) paid for by long term revenues (leases). Unbalanced financial structures which funded site operations with property sales revenue had led to severe problems in other cities when the local real estate markets periodically dried up. A bond issue provides an early "market check" for projects expected to get a substantial proportion of their investment from the private sector. Other public authorities will have to provide well-defined future revenue streams to sell bonds, since the municipal market was closed to "moral obligation" funding after the 1975 New York fiscal crisis and defaults by other agencies in the 1980's [Axelrod 1992; Mitchell and Miller 1992].

The early political and planning problems meant that the BPCA missed the opportunity to get developers to invest in the site during the relatively good years between 1966 and 1971.

After the office market collapsed in 1972, the BPCA was only able to attract Harry Helmsley to the site if he did not have to invest his own money and he withdrew during the next recession. The BPCA signed up its first residential developer in 1973, just past the peak of the residential market (Figure 36) and was forced to *pay* Lefrak and Fisher management fees to stay on the site through the recession. However, the reconstituted agency proved quite adept at capturing private investment during the 1980's. The cyclical nature of the real estate market means that the window of opportunity for a redevelopment agency may only be open for a year or two near the peak of each cycle. Richard Kahan moved quite quickly to attract commercial development to the site in 1980, signing up Olympia and York within a year of working out a new plan with New York City.

O & Y obtained all the approvals and started construction within another year. A six month delay would have pushed the project into the 1982 recession so that financing (and tenants) might not have been available (Figure 37). The agency had a strategic advantage because it had compressed its developer selection process and the municipal approval process so that they could get construction going within one market cycle. Developers, like those selected for Rector Place, usually delay negotiations through a recession, in order to avoid commitments to build when construction financing and customers are not available. Misjudging the market cycle can be frustrating for an agency and disastrous for a developer, as Olympia and York discovered when they went bankrupt trying to develop Canary Wharf in London (Figure 37).

The BPCA reduced some of the impact of real estate market cycles on its operations by using long term land leases rather than fee simple sales of property. A lease provides a steady stream of income while the timing of cash sales fluctuates with the real estate market. The London Docklands Development Corporation's income from property sales declined precipitously in 1990, when the banks stopped lending to developers. The BPCA's property income actually increased from 1988 to 1991 as the escalation clauses in the World Financial Center leases kicked in (Appendix A). These participating leases smoothed out the peaks of the boom and provided increased funding during the early 1990's recession. Participating leases also allowed the

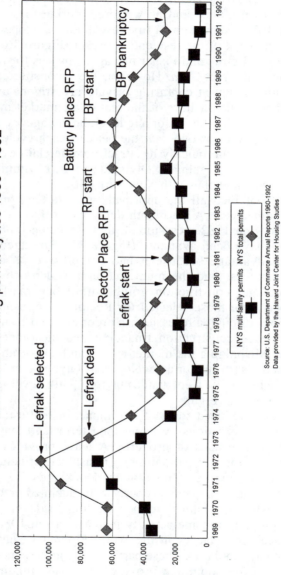

Figure 36 New York Residential Market Cycles.
Source: Data Provided by Harvard Joint Centre for Housing Studies.

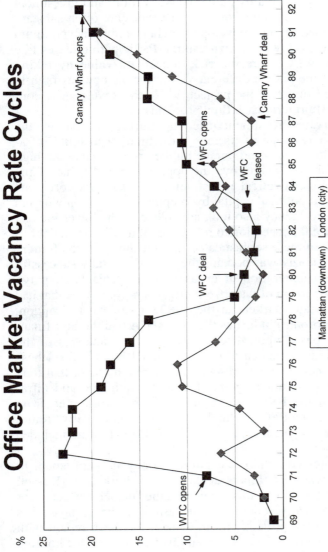

Figure 37 New York Office Market Cycles.
Source: Data from Coldwell Banker 1994.

Sources: Coldwell Banker 1994; Herring Baker Harris 1992; Jones Lang Wooten 1993; Solomon Brothers 1991.

agency to attract developers with low base costs during the uncertain start-up period, but participate in the long term appreciation of value created by public land assembly and investment [Sagalyn 1993]. Revenue from property sales are often substantially discounted because developers include a high risk premium and may have to use their own capital. Participating leases like those in the WFC share the risk and create value by taking advantage of the parties different views: the agency has faith in the long term future of the project, while the developer is concerned with short term cash flow problems.

When private investment dried up during recessions, the BPCA took advantage of its long term funding to build infrastructure at low prices and pursue public projects, (like the high school) which would improve the appearance and value of the site. The counter cyclical investments also kept its core staff intact and built political capital by keeping construction workers employed. The agency also took advantage of the lower interest rates in the 1990's recession to refinance all its long term debt.

As a result of these sophisticated fiscal techniques, the Battery Park City Authority was perhaps the most financially successful of the current generation of urban renewal projects [Sagalyn 1993]. A comparison of waterfront projects in four cities that had strong real estate markets in the 1980's (New York, London, Boston and Toronto) indicates that the BPCA had the best financial returns, based upon discounted cash flow analysis of the agencies' annual financial reports [Gordon 1997b]. All of these projects had negative net present values, which meant that they needed their government grants for land acquisition and infrastructure, but the BPCA came closest to breaking even from 1968 to 1992. The BPCA actually showed a small positive return by 1992 when Payments in Lieu of Taxes (PILOT) were included in the analysis.

When critics complain that public money is being spent to subsidize private developers at the Battery Park City [Russell 1994; Boyer 1994] they misunderstand the financial structure of the project. Actually, relatively little cash from the taxpayers has been spent on the project, and most of it has been repaid with interest. Substantial sums have been diverted to renovate housing in needy neighborhoods and reduce the City's deficit, and hundreds of millions of dollars more are planned.

A more telling critique is that the BPCA is financed with "off balance sheet" tax expenditures:

- tax-free municipal bonds
- "moral guarantees" by the state of the 1972 bonds
- federal mortgage insurance of the Gateway Plaza bonds
- payments in lieu of property taxes
- property tax abatements from New York City.

These tactics are certainly public subsidies and conceal the size of the public deficit. They also make the public authorities who use them harder to control since they are outside the usual budgetary control of legislatures [Axelrod 1992; Sagalyn 1992, Walsh 1990).

Although there may be some concerns about their indirect impacts, the relatively sophisticated financial techniques used by the BPCA dramatically reduced the cash contribution by their sponsor, the New York state government, and launched some substantial public benefits. With increasing fiscal constraints at all levels of government, grants for redevelopment projects are likely to become a distant memory. Battery Park City may be setting the example for funding high-priority projects in the future.

Planning, Design and Managing Change

Battery Park City has been a laboratory for the transition from Modern architecture to Post-Modern urban design. When the UDC took over the BPCA in 1979, Richard Kahan quipped that the many site models in the boardroom reminded him of the Hall of Dinosaurs at a museum. The early schemes looked a bit like Le Corbusier's Plan Voisin placed on a barge moored to Manhattan. The 1969 plan, launched in the year of the moon landing, was surely seen as a space station tethered to the island. Moshe Safdie tried his Habitat from the 1967 World's Fair. Only Sam Lefrak's systems-built apartment buildings at Gateway Plaza emerged from those days.

The BPCA tried to implement the 1969 plan for a decade, but it just would not start. The plan might have worked if more working capital was available and the entire project was subsidized housing built by the agency. However, the high proportion of offices and luxury housing meant that private developers would be involved. The megastructure was fundamentally unsuited for implementation in stages by several builders, and the large up-front costs of the spine caused the agency and developers to delay the construction of the infrastructure.

The 1979 plan was a turning point in North American urban design. Cooper and Eckstut demonstrated the use of traditional infrastructure – streets and parks – to shape urban space. The rhetoric about extending the Manhattan street grid into the site collided with the 10 lane reality of the West Side Highway, and Battery Park City remains somewhat isolated from the rest of the city [Strickland 1991; Posner 1989]. However, the at-grade connections planned at the north and south ends of the site should help make access more normal.

Cooper and Eckstut were quickly offered other significant urban design commissions [Doubilet 1986] where they elaborated upon the techniques they developed at Battery Park City. Stanton Eckstut summarized the approach:

1. Think Small. *Plan in increments, with many architects. Avoid the construction camp appearance by completing one phase at a time.*

2. Learn From What Exists. *Reuse existing buildings, where possible, and get clues from the site and surrounding areas.*

3. Integrate. *Avoid platforms and build at grade to integrate with streets. Connect to the water.*

4. Design Streets, Not Buildings. *Promote activity on commercial streets. Use design guidelines to foster coherence in the public realm. [Eckstut 1986b].*

These techniques proved to be quite practical for implementation, and they also incorporated the influence of urban history, sociology and place studies, particularly the observations of Jane Jacobs [1961]. The incremental approach had many benefits. The hand of many architects creates a diverse feel and a finer grain for a project, which eliminates the monotony of many previous efforts at urban renewal. The finer grain also allowed smaller developers to get involved, which encouraged a broader market for the land, and better financial returns. It was also politically savvy, since the work was spread around and there were many opportunities for politicians to demonstrate accomplishments.

A good development phasing plan can reduce costs and improve the image of the site during implementation. Proper phasing allows infrastructure to be extended on an incremental basis and each neighborhood to be completely furnished, so the project minimizes its "construction site" appearance. The Battery Park City Authority took advantage of its completely clear site (a vacant landfill) to phase its development perfectly. It started from the most advantageous point adjacent to the existing city, the World Trade Center, and expanded outward on a contiguous basis, one parcel at a time (Figure 38). Starting in the center means that the site has two un-built edges, but it also doubles the number of contiguous parcels available when development recommences after a recession. These edges are somewhat finished, since the agency has built the streets which define the parcels.

The design guidelines were part of a deliberate strategy to encourage quality in the built environment by using the developer selection process. Rather than simply holding an auction for the land, the BPCA published guidelines which gave considerable guidance about the character of the future precinct and demonstrated their commitment by building the public spaces. Potential developers recognized that they needed talented architects for the buildings, but the guidelines were specific enough about built form that they had some confidence in the financial projections in their proposals. Olympia and York were able to bid on the office complex on the basis of the guidelines. They later ran a limited design competition, thus separating the financial and design issues for this important site.

Not everyone was happy with the new approach. Some architects, (particularly those with a modernist approach) chafed under the restraints of the urban design guidelines, or felt that it was inappropriate to use older precedents in a modern development [Posner 1989; Strickland 1991; Russell 1994]. They ignored the marketing appeal of the buildings. The potential residents were comforted by the feel of the traditional, successful New York neighborhoods in a situation where they were pioneers settling a new district. There are no outstanding buildings

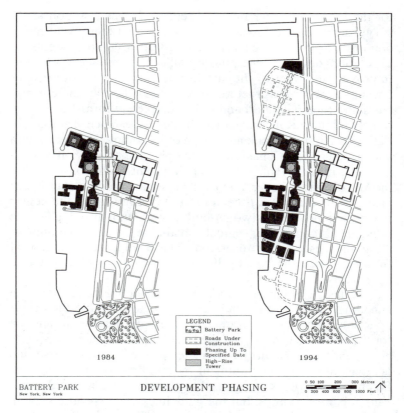

Figure 38   Battery Park City Phasing.
Source: Based on Battery Park City Authority.

in Rector Place but it is appropriate that no buildings should stand out, since the private residences act as "background buildings" to the focal point at the World Financial Center. In secular, late 20th century lower Manhattan, the dominance of the skyline by financial corporations appears to reflect the social structure as clearly as the churches of 18th century Rome.

The World Financial Center was hailed as the second coming of the Rockefeller Center by local critics [Huxtable 1981; Goldberger 1983a; Dean 1986] who were perhaps bored with all the flat-topped corporate boxes produced during the 1960's and 1970's. After the decorative excesses of the post-modern sky-

scrapers of the late 1980's, Cesar Pelli's design now seems a
rather quiet and dignified scheme. The proportions of the buildings are a bit squat, the dual effect of the height limits and the
large trading floors demanded by the investment banks [Posner
1989]. With six million square feet in the program, there must
have been a strong temptation to try to dominate the skyline, in
the manner of the World Trade Center, or the seventy story
complex proposed at the south end of the 1969 plan. Instead, the
main guidelines of the 1979 plan were simple – the complex was
to be no more than 15.0 FAR and half the height of the World
Trade Center. These guidelines were essentially modest, by the
standards of New York skyscrapers. Pelli's design actually
improves the appearance of the two brute towers of the World
Trade Center on the skyline while restoring some semblance of
scale to the west side of lower Manhattan (Figure 39).

Of course, the buildings are only a part of Cooper and
Eckstut's plan, and not even the most important part. The BPCA
adopted a comprehensive strategy of changing the poor image of
their waterfront site through high quality public spaces and institutions. The agency built these places in advance of the private
development, clearly delivering the promised public benefits and
building political capital with the City. The parks, public art and
institutions also created confidence among the potential private
developers about the quality of the neighborhood they were
invited to invest in. The agency followed up by maintaining
these spaces at a standard far higher than the unfortunate norm in
New York these days.

The public has responded by flocking to the esplanade and
parks in droves, and many of the reviews have been almost rap-
turous [Starr 1993; Gill 1990; Goldberger 1990; Wiseman 1986].
All this praise has elevated the project to the status of a 'sacred
cow' and produced a backlash. The academic left became almost
vituperative in the criticism [Boyer 1994, 1991; Russell 1994;
Deutsche 1991; Fainstein 1994]. They regard Battery Park City
as an inauthentic New York experience – it is too clean, too safe,
too stable, and not gritty enough to reflect the chaos of the
current urban society:

> ... an urban life too "purified" ... of all those unde-
> sirable elements which lurk in the sometimes psy-
> chotic urban environment. Unfortunately, these are

Figure 39 Battery Park City 1995.
Source: Battery Bark City Authority.

*inseparable from the 'exhilarating' aspects of human
life. Existence in Battery Park City will be very
pleasant, but it will never constitute the same kind of
rich urban milieu that makes Manhattan what it is.
[Russell 1994:208]*

Many New Yorkers have had quite enough exhilaration from
their "sometimes psychotic urban environment", and they cite
crime as the most important reason why they want to leave the
city. Other quality of life issues such as dirt, battered parks and
crumbling streets are also high on their list [Vitullo-Martin
1993]. It is no crime to enjoy public spaces which are safe, clean
and delight the senses. New York needs more of these suppos-
edly inauthentic places.

A more serious charge is that the public spaces in Battery Park
City are private places for rich white people, policed by security
guards. The privatization of public spaces is a serious concern
[Sorkin 1992], but Battery Park City is no simulation of Main
Street in the manner of shopping malls or Disneyland. The
streets and parks are owned by the City, maintained by a public
authority and policed by City park rangers. Everyone is allowed
access on the same basis as they are to public parks. In the
hundreds of hours I have spent in the neighborhood, I have only
seen one person hustled away by the guards – a (white, male)
rollerblader trying to skate through the cafes at the Winter
Garden. One older man rummaging through the garbage cans
confided to me that he was going to try another spot, as the pick-
ings were slim because the bins were emptied so frequently.

A more telling criticism of the early public spaces was that too
much emphasis was placed upon aesthetic criteria, and not
enough attention to the needs of local users, especially children
[Hoelterhoff 1988]. This issue came to a boil with the South
Gardens controversy, and the BPCA was forced to include the
residents in the design process for the Hudson River Park and
Wagner Park. These two spaces are less formal than those in the
center of the site, and programmed for more use by local residents (large and small) without sacrificing the high quality and
public art characteristic of the rest of the site.

The BPCA and the City of New York spent more than a decade
struggling over the redevelopment of the site. They were only
able to step back from their adversarial positions after Rockefeller

and Lindsay had left the scene and their replacements were faced with the mutual disaster of bankruptcy and a default of the bonds. With the harsh light of impending failure upon them in November 1979, Richard Kahan and Robert Wagner Jr. were able to put aside the entrenched positions of their governments and negotiate an arrangement which disentangled their roles and gave each side what it needed to get on with the job. The City agreed to help the agency develop the site: it gave up the land, arranged property tax incentives, a fast approval process for the commercial node, and allowed the agency some flexibility in the development of the site. The state agreed to a plan that fit the City's urban design approach, guaranteed the benefits associated with the public realm and provided bridge financing.

The trade-off between development flexibility and public certainty was accommodated with satisfactory results by an incremental urban design approach which focused upon the quality of public space. Detailed guidelines for the massing and the use of the buildings are set not by the city, but by the implementation agency, just before they went to the market for investment. These techniques allow the agency to make minor adjustments to the massing and use within an overall envelope approved by a master plan, while giving the government some certainty about the quality and extent of the public realm. This approach proved to be influential both for waterfronts and other urban redevelopment projects [Dixon 1993; *Time* 1990; Barnett 1987]. The term "the new urbanism" is perhaps more appropriate for Battery Park City than Seaside, Florida.

Of course, the Battery Park City model for implementation may not be replicated automatically elsewhere. New York City abandoned the traditional regulatory role in planning and depended upon the BPCA for quality control of public spaces and private buildings, a task that the agency has executed superbly to date [Fisher 1988:92]. Ironically, the city got a better outcome by conceding authority than it usually gets from its normal planning process, but it depended upon public officials who insisted upon first rate design, even as the project faced bankruptcy. Not every redevelopment agency has recognized and developed the connection between quality spaces, future land value and political support, but if the results as Battery Park City are a guide, they should consider this strategy.

EPILOG

Almost three decades after the Nelson Rockefeller and John Lindsay took their boat tour on the Hudson River, the best way to visit Battery Park City is still by water. Although the great ocean liners have largely vanished, the ferries from Hoboken now provide a fine view. The evening trip is glorious, when the entire island is lit by the golden light of sunset. Ironically, New Jersey residents have the best entrance to a pet project of the Governor of New York.

If you chug across the river in the morning, the project does not stand out, since Battery Park City does not dominate the back-lit skyline of Lower Manhattan. It fits into the city and even makes the mute towers of the World Trade Center look like they belong. As the ferry swings along the un-built north neighborhood of the site, you might notice something unusual: hundreds of people enjoying the parks and esplanade, even though the proposed buildings are not completed yet.

The ferry docks near the World Financial Center, and the commuters disappear for the office buildings downtown. A visitor might sit in an outdoor cafe, or stroll the Esplanade to Battery Park. If the weather is poor, you could slip into the Winter Garden and relax at one of the tables in that soaring space.

In the evening, the commuters pour down the grand staircase in the Winter Garden. The stream splits to exit by the doors on either edge of the glass wall overlooking the harbor. The commuters seem unaffected by the quality and scale of the space, like the thousands who flow through the main concourse at Grand Central Station every day. When the current of harried humanity hits the water's edge it seems to hesitate a bit. People slow down; ties are loosened; comfortable sneakers appear from handbags; jackets are removed. The inevitable few who miss

115

the ferry shrug their shoulders; another will be along in a few
minutes. Curiously, they don't crowd into the waiting area at the
dock like the frantic subway riders. Some settle in along the
esplanade railing to watch the traffic on the river. The human
stream along the walkway is just as fascinating to others – the
joggers, rollerbladers, parents pushing children, dogs pulling
owners, seniors out for a stroll.

What brings them together? A few may live here, but that
can't account for the crowd. Battery Park City is simply a clean,
safe and attractive downtown neighborhood, with waterfront
views which calm the human spirit and, perhaps, enrich the soul.
In a city of abandoned buildings, graffiti, run-down parks and
pervasive fear, it is both a ray of sunshine and beacon of hope.
For planners, designers and politicians, it is an affirmation. With
skill, a bit of luck and attention to the best features of urban life,
we can still get it right.

Battery Park City Chronology

Sources

[NYT]   *New York Times*, (generally reported the day after the item).

[1]   Bellush, J. and R. Netzer. 1990. *Urban Politics New York Style*, New York: Sharpe, pp. 429–445.

[2]   Frederick O'R. Hayes, "Battery Park City Development History," Working Draft, Frederick O'R. Hayes Associates, July 1, 1986.

[3]   New York State Office of the State Comptroller, "Audit Report on the Financial and Operating Status of the Battery Park City Authority," Division of Audits and Accounts, Report No. NY-Auth-24–76.

[4]   Sagalyn, L.S. "Draft Chronology of Battery Park City Development," Revised February 2, 1991.

[5]   New York State Assembly Committee on Housing, "Battery Park City Authority – A Time For Decision," February 15, 1979.

[6]   S.L. Fordsham, "World Financial Center," *Urban Land*, Vol. 44, No. 9 (September 1985), pp. 22–26.

Abbreviations

BOE	New York City Board of Estimate
BPC	Battery Park City
BPCA	Battery Park City Authority
CPC	City Planning Commission
DLMA	Downtown-Lower Manhattan Association
EFCB	Emergency Financial Control Board
FHA	US Federal Housing Administration
HNYC	Housing New York Corporation
HUD	US Department of Housing and Urban Development
LMP	Lower Manhattan Plan
MDP	Master Development Plan
MOU	Memorandum of Understanding
NYC/S	New York City/State
NYDMA	New York City Department of Marine and Aviation
NYMEX	New York Mercantile Exchange
NYT	New York Times

OLMD	Office of Lower Manhattan Development
O&Y	Olympia & York developers
RFP	Request for proposals
S&P	Standard and Poors
STOL	Short Take-off and Landing
UDC	NY State Urban Development Corporation
WFC	World Financial Center

Prior to 1992

October 14, 1958	The Downtown-Lower Manhattan Association, led by David Rockefeller, releases a plan for redevelopment of lower Manhattan and the East River waterfront [NYT]
November 1958	Nelson Rockefeller (Republican) is elected governor of the State of New York [1]
January 1960	DLMA proposes a World Trade Center on the East River waterfront
November 1960	Massachusetts Senator John F. Kennedy (Democrat) elected President [1]
November 1961	Robert F. Wagner (Democrat) is elected to a third term as mayor [1]
1962	Hudson River waterfront studies initiated by NYC, at the request of Governor Rockefeller [2]
November 1962	Nelson Rockefeller is re-elected governor [1]
1963	
April 25, 1963	Proposal by NYDMA for Hudson waterfront with apartments, industrial and cargo facilities [NYT]
November 21, 1963	DLMA releases a plan for the downtown, including residential redevelopment on the Hudson River
1964	
September 21, 1964	Alternative Hudson River proposal issued by City Planning Commission (CPC) [NYT]
November 1964	President Johnson re-elected in a landslide with a Democratic-controlled Congress [1]
1965	
February 23, 1965	New York CPC staff start a new plan for Lower Manhattan [NYT]
November 1965	U.S. Rep. John V. Lindsay is elected mayor, on the Republican and Liberal Party tickets [1]
December 30, 1965	Draft Lower Manhattan Plan released on last day of Wagner administration [NYT]
1966	
May 12, 1966	Governor Nelson Rockefeller announces "Battery Park City" plan [NYT]

June 22, 1966	Lower Manhattan Plan (LMP) released by the City [NYT]
November 1966	Nelson Rockefeller is re-elected Governor [1]
November 18, 1966	NYDMA proposes a STOL airport for the BPC site [NYT]
December 20, 1966	The Waterside complex for the East River proposed by Mayor Lindsay [NYT]
December 23, 1966	Port Authority awards contract for BPC landfill [NYT]
1967	
January 18, 1967	City creates the Office of Lower Manhattan Development (OLMD) to implement the LMP [NYT]
June 11, 1967	Half-mile high space needle proposed for Battery Park by the CPC [NYT]
November 1967	DLMA releases a market study recommending luxury and middle income housing for BPC
1968	NY State creates the Urban Development Corporation [UDC] [1]
April 25, 1968	Rockefeller and Lindsay announce BPC Memorandum of Understanding (MOU) [NYT]
May 31, 1968	State legislation to set up BPC Corporation enacted [2]
August 5, 1968	Charles J. Urstadt elected chairman of BPCA [NYT]
September 1968	Urstadt negotiates $600,000 start up funding from two banks [NYT]
November 1968	Former Vice-President (1953–61) Richard Nixon elected President [1]
April 15, 1969	International Longshoreman's Union sues the BPCA [NYT]
1969	
April 16, 1969	City and State architects complete the Master Development Plan for BPC
May 23, 1969	DLMA releases "Planning for Lower Manhattan" report, supporting the new Master Plan for BPC
Summer 1969	Mayor Lindsay loses Republican nomination for re-election, runs as Liberal Party candidate
June 30, 1969	Liberal Democrats demand changes to BPC housing mix in exchange for supporting Lindsay [NYT]
May 21, 1969	Battery Park City Corporation name changed to Battery Park City Authority [2]
August 15, 1969	Mayor Lindsay reverses his stand on BPC housing and supports 1/3 low-income units [NYT]
August 20, 1969	Zoning changes approved by CPC and BOE after no opposition
October 9, 1969	Special Battery Park District zoning approved by Board of Estimate [NYT]

Fall 1969	Economic recession begins and the city's economy goes into a slow decline [1]
November 1969	Lindsay re-elected mayor as Liberal party nominee, after losing the Republican primary [1]
November 24, 1969	Master Lease with NYC incorporating the Master Development Plan (MDP) signed [3]

1970

July 1970	First demolition, Pier 19 [2]
Sept.–Dec. 1970	BPCA advertises for office leases without success [NYT]
October 1970	Basic engineering studies of the site begin [NYT]
November 1970	Rockefeller is elected to a fourth term as governor [1]
1971	First tower of the World Trade Center is occupied, absorbing much of the downtown office market
April 16, 1971	BPCA advertises for residential developers [NYT]
June 1, 1971	NYS assembly caps BPCA borrowing capacity at $300 million [4]
August 1971	Lindsay seeks the Democratic presidential nomination, but withdraws after poor primary results [1]
August 1971	Construction of bulkheads and landfill related to a 16-acre section placed under contract [2]
August 29, 1971	West Side Highway proposal announced by UDC. BPCA objects [NYT]
October 19, 1971	First amendment to the Master Lease specifies procedures for resolving property tax disputes

1972

January 5, 1972	Harry Helmsley selected as office developer for BPC [2]
January 25, 1972	US Corps of Engineers issues permits for BPC landfill [2]
April 12, 1972	Mayor Lindsay and David Rockefeller unveil the Manhattan Landing waterfront plan [NYT]
May 1, 1972	1972 BPC bond offering for $200 million
June 28, 1972	Urstadt objects to Manhattan Landing and requests cuts in low income units at BPC [NYT]
July 15, 1972	Amendment to the MDP reducing low-income housing to 20% [2]
November 1972	President Nixon is re-elected. The Democrats win control of both houses of Congress [1]
1973	Lefrak and Fisher sign letter of intent to develop housing and shopping center
June 5, 1973	State Assembly authorizes the extension of the project area north to approximately Jay Street [4]
June 11, 1973	BPCA gets various powers for construction and financing of subsidized housing [4]

July 1973	Revised master plan by Harrison & Abramovitz reviewed by CPC [NYT]
November 1973	City Comptroller Abraham Beame (Democrat) is elected mayor [1]
November 14, 1973	MDP amendment substitutes Special BPC District Zoning and prohibits low-income housing buildings [4]
December 1973	Governor Rockefeller resigns to head a federal commission. He is succeeded by Lt. Gov. M. Wilson [1]
1974	City building permits for 1624 middle-income housing units (Lefrak) issued
June 18, 1974	Second Amendment to the Master Lease, to make BPC more competitive with Manhattan Landing [4]
August 1974	President Nixon resigns. VP Gerald Ford succeeds him, and appoints former Nelson Rockefeller VP
September 20, 1974	"Ground Breaking Ceremony" at BPC. Piles are driven for Pod III [NYT]
October 23, 1974	Third Amendment to the Master Lease, incorporating major changes to plan and review process [2]
October 24, 1974	Fourth Amendment to the Master Lease, increasing the site to approximately 100 acres [4]
Fall 1974	There is increasing difficulty in selling New York City notes to the bond market [1] A national credit crunch and deepening recession threaten the credit of state agencies
November 1974	Conflict between BPCA architects and Lefrak reported [NYT] U.S. Representative Hugh Carey is elected governor, defeating Malcolm Wilson [1]
1975	BPC a contending site for the City's new convention center
January 1975	Default by the UDC on a bond payment, inducing a State fiscal crisis
Spring 1975	New York City has no access to the credit markets, inducing a city budget crisis [1]
April 15, 1975	BPCA hits UDC-induced snag in planned bond issue for middle-income housing units [NYT]
June 1975	The Municipal Assistance Corporation is created by the State [1]
September 1975	The state takes formal control over city finances using the Emergency Financial Control Board [1] BPCA made subject to EFCB procedures for review and approval of spending [NYT] BPCA applies for FHA insurance backing bonds for middle-income housing [NYT]

November 1975	President Ford and Congress authorize seasonal loans to the City over the next three years
1976	Landfill operations completed [2]
February 5, 1976	BPCA selects Starrett Housing and the National Kinney second phase housing developers [NYT]
February 20, 1976	State Comptroller Levitt files audit report on BPCA's financial and operating status [3]
April 1, 1976	State caps the general bond-issuing authority and cuts housing bonds to $85 million [2]
November 1976	Democrat Jimmy Carter narrowly defeats Gerald Ford in the Presidential election [1] HUD-FHA task force formed to review BPCA's request for $65 million in mortgage insurance [2]
Late 1976	The worst cutbacks completed and the city's finances have stabilized. State assumes some city functions [1]
1977	
November 1977	U.S. Rep. Edward I. Koch (Democrat) is elected mayor, defeating incumbent Beame in the primary [1]
1978	
January 10, 1978	NYS Assembly Housing Committee votes to conduct a review of BPCA [NYT]
March 23, 1978	Construction workers break up State Assembly meeting with BPCA chaired by Edward Lehner [NYT]
May 12, 1978	FHA issues a conditional commitment for $68.5 million housing insurance [5]
Fall 1978	BOE grants tax exemption for POD-3 housing which was required by BPCA [5] EFCB approves $2.9 million in BPCA capital expenditures for roads and utilities [5]
September 14, 1978	Fifth amendment to the Master Lease. Waiver of payments from BPCA to NYC
September 27, 1978	State Comptroller's report on BPCA. Affirms the concept as a public endeavor [BPCA 1978]
November 1978	Democrat Hugh Carey is re-elected governor, with Mario Cuomo as Lt. Governor [1]
1979	An office construction boom that continues until 1990, begins in Manhattan [1]
January 5, 1979	Governor Carey uses recess appointments to take control of BPCA Board and removes Urstadt [NYT]
February 10, 1979	Richard Kahan, chairman of UDC, also appointed BPCA President [NYT]
February 15, 1979	NY State Assembly (Lehner) report calls for retrenchment in BPCA's role as a public developer

April 9, 1979	NY State Assembly Committee on Legislative Oversight report predicts 1980 BPCA bond default
April 24, 1979	DLMA releases its study recommending a State rescue of the project [Vollmer Associates 1979]
October 28, 1979	NY State Budget Office "work out plan" for Battery Park City released
October 31, 1979	New BPC master plan by Alexander Cooper Assoc. proposed major changes in land uses and urban design
November 8, 1979	Memorandum of Understanding among the City, the State and BPCA signed, committing major changes in planning and development of the site
December 17, 1979	CPC approves the deal and new planning regulations for the commercial complex

1980

May 17, 1980	HUD-FHA insurance finally obtained; S&P rates the bonds AAA [NYT]
June 6, 1980	Settlement Agreement signed by City, State and BPCA
June 10, 1980	Sixth amendment to the Master Lease, implementing the Settlement Agreement [2]
June 1980	Gateway Plaza housing construction begun [2]
July 1, 1980	Developer RFP for commercial sites sent out to 30 developers; 12 submissions [2]
October 10, 1980	American Stock Exchange drops BPC site location due to rising costs [NYT]
November 1980	Ronald Reagan (Republican) defeats Jimmy Carter for the presidency [1]
November 13, 1980	Designation of O&Y to undertake entire commercial development, to start in 1981 and finish in 1985

1981

1981–1982	The Federal Reserve's successful effort to end inflation by monetary stringency leads to an even more severe recession that in 1974–75 [6]
March 1981	O&Y and American Express sign letter of intent for one tower [2]
April 1981	RFP for 2200-unit Rector Place; 27 submissions
May 13, 1981	O&Y announce design plans and 1987 completion date for the World Financial Center [NYT]
May 24, 1981	Ada Louise Huxtable hails the WFC plan as "a new Rockefeller Center" [NYT]
August 18, 1981	Developers chosen for Rector Place housing sites [NYT]
September 1981	Master ground lease between O&Y and BPCA signed

November 1981	Koch is re-elected mayor with both the Democratic and Republican party nominations [1]
December 1981	O&Y begins construction on the World Financial Center [NYT]

1982

1982–1985	The local economy is booming. The city begins to rebuild its infrastructure and housing
June 1982	Gateway Plaza housing (Pod III) opens; first site residents move in [2]
October 21, 1982	BPCA's lease with O&Y amended to accommodate changes for O&Y's financing [NYT]
November 1982	Mario Cuomo is elected governor after defeating Mayor Edward Koch in the Democratic primary [1]

1983

January 15, 1983	Gateway Plaza tenants hold a rent strike [NYT]
June 15, 1983	O&Y master sublease replaced by separate severance leases for each of four parcels [4]
June 16, 1983	O&Y enters into leasehold arrangement for Parcel C with American Express [NYT] Merrill Lynch agreements for B&D buildings
June 29, 1983	First phase of the Esplande officially opens [NYT]
October 1983	O&Y's first financing after 22 months of internal financing of construction – $728 million short-term loan from Manufacturers Hannover Trust and 21 international banks [6]

1984

January 1, 1984	Richard Kahan, Chairman and Barry Light, President of BPCA resign, after request by Governor Cuomo Meyer S. Frucher appointed President
Spring 1984	Leases finally signed with developers for Rector Place residential neighborhood [2]
April 1984	Construction of Rector Place begun [2]
Aug 1984	O&Y and Merrill Lynch sign 3,000 page document covering their office space deal [NYT]
Dec 1984	O&Y's $728 million construction loan restructured [2]

1985

May 23, 1985	Koch and Cuomo sign Memorandum of Understanding to use excess BPCA revenues for low- and moderate-income housing in the Housing New York program
October 1985	Occupancy of WFC buildings 1 & 2 [NYT October 19, 1985]

| November 1985 | Koch is re-elected mayor by a wide margin [1] |

1986

1986–1988	The city's bond rating is increased to its highest level since 1975 [1]
Late 1980s	The longest unbroken economic upsurge on record (from the recession of 1982) [1]
March 1986	NYS Legislature and Governor reach agreement on housing program [NYT March 19, 1986]
August 15, 1986	Amendment to the 1979 Settlement Agreement. Major change to State/City relationship [4]
August 20, 1986	Oppenheimer Lease at WFC announced [NYT]
August 22, 1986	BPCA issues $184,850,000 in Special Obligation Bonds [4] Housing New York Program legislation passed [4]
November 1986	Cuomo is re-elected governor [1]

1987

| October 1, 1987 | $209,995,000 HNYC Bonds issued for low and moderate income housing |

1988

July 1988	South Cove park opens [NYT]
October 5, 1988	David Emil announced as new President of BPCA [NYT]
October 15, 1988	Winter Garden at WFC opens [NYT]
1989	Economic growth in the city stops. Budget retrenchment begins in the fall [1]
June 15, 1989	"Agreement for Certain Payments" signed allocating BPCA excess revenues to State and City
June 15, 1989	Infrastructure Agreement provides for bonding of $68.5 million to build out project [4]
November 1989	Former Manhattan Borough President David Dinkins (Democrat) is elected mayor
December 30, 1989	Financial agreement allows BPCA funds to be used to deal with City budget shortfalls [4] Memorandum of Understanding between City and BPCA signed regarding Hotel and Holocaust Museum [4]

1990

May 31, 1990	BPCA issues $222,660,000 in Revenue Bonds for City budget relief [4]
June 6, 1990	Settlement Agreement between City and BPCA signed regarding excess revenues [4]
November 1990	Mario Cuomo (Democrat) re-elected as Governor of New York State

1991

October 1991   Governor Cuomo cancels the South Garden park after a lengthy design controversy [NYT]

1992

June 1992   Hudson River Park opens after redesign with extensive community participation [NYT]

November 3, 1992   Democrat William Clinton defeats incumbent President George Bush [NYT]

1993

Fall 1993   BPCA RFP for developers for four sites in the North Neighborhood [BPCA 1994]

October 1993   NYC Department of City Planning releases the "Plan for Lower Manhattan" report

November 2, 1993   Republican Rudolph Giuliani defeats incumbent David Dinkins to become NYC mayor

December 16, 1993   BPCA issues $850 million in bonds to refinance all its debt at lower interest rates [BPCA 1994]

1994   BPCA issues design guidelines for the North Neighborhood [NYT]

August 1994   BPCA releases the Lower Manhattan Urban Design Plan New York Mercantile Exchange agrees to relocate to BPC [BPCA 1994a]
Holocaust Museum lease signed [BPCA 1994a]

October 18, 1994   Ground-breaking ceremony for the Holocaust Museum [NYT]

November 8, 1994   Republican George E. Pataki defeats incumbent Mario Cuomo to become NY State Governor [NYT]

November 14, 1994   Philip Pitruzzello appointed BPCA President after resignation of David Emil
BPCA designates three developers for the North Neighborhood

December 15, 1994   Mayor Giuliani proposes economic and zoning incentives for Lower Manhattan development

1995   Lease with NY Mercantile Exchange (NYMEX) signed for Site 15

March 1995   BPCA issues design guidelines for Site 15, adjacent to the WFC

Bibliography

Abramovitz, Max, 1992. Architect. Interviewed by David Gordon, June 24.

Axelrod, D. 1992. *Shadow Government: The hidden world of public authorities and how they control $1 trillion of your money*, New York: John Wiley.

Barnett, J. 1974. *Urban Design as Public Policy: Practical Methods for Improving Cities*, New York: Architectural Record Books.

Barnett, J. 1974. *Urban Design as Public Policy: Practical Methods for Improving Cities*, New York: Architectural Record Books.

Barnett, J. 1982. *An Introduction to Urban Design*, New York: Harper & Row.

Barnett, J. 1987. "In the Public Interest: Design Guidelines," *Architectural Record*, July, pp. 114–25.

Battery Park City Authority, 1972. *Series A Bonds Official Statement*, New York: BPCA, May 1.

Battery Park City Authority, 1979. *Memorandum of Understanding between NYS, NYC, UDC, & BPCA*. Dated November 8.

Battery Park City Authority, 1989. "Agreement and Consent with the City of New York" dated December 30.

Battery Park City Authority, 1990b. *Revenue Bonds, Series 1990 Official Statement*, New York: BPCA, May 31.

Battery Park City Authority, 1993. *Annual Report 1992–93*, New York: BPCA.

Battery Park City Authority, 1994a. *Annual Report 1993–94*, New York: BPCA.

Battery Park City Authority, 1994b. *Design Guidelines for the North Residential Neighborhood*, New York: BPCA. Consultants: Ralph Lerner Architect, Alexander Gorlin Architect, Machado and Silvetti Associates.

Belfer, Linda, 1992. Gateway Plaza resident, Chair, BPC Committee Manhattan Community Board No. 1. Interviewed by David Gordon, June 24.

Bellush, J. & R. Netzer, (eds.), 1990. *Urban Politics New York Style*, New York: Sharpe.

Bleeker, S.E. 1981. *The Politics of Architecture: A Perspective on Nelson Rockefeller*, New York: Rutledge.

Boyer, M.C. 1994. *The City of Collective Memory: Its Historical Imagery and Architectural Entertainments*, Cambridge MA: MIT Press.

Boyer, M.C. 1988. "The Return of Aesthetics to City Planning," *Society*, May/June, pp. 49–57.

Breen, A. & D. Rigby, 1993. Urban Waterfronts: Cities Reclaim Their Edge, New York: McGraw-Hill.

Brutomesso, R. 1993. *Waterfronts: A New Frontier For Cities On Water*, Venice: International Centre Cities on Water.

Burden, Amanda, 1992. Vice President Design, BPCA. Interviewed by David Gordon, June 24.

Carroll, Maurice, 1966. "Downtown Plan Widely Praised," *New York Times*, June 23, p. 78.

Cooper, A. 1979. *Battery Park City Draft Summary Report and 1979 Master Plan*, New York: BPCA, October.

Cooper, A. 1979. *Battery Park City Draft Summary Report and 1979 Master Plan*, New York: BPCA, October.

Cooper, Alexander, 1986. Architect and Urban Designer. Interviewed by Frederick Hayes, August 20.

Cushman & Wakefield, 1995. *Downtown New York Office Market Report: First Quarter 1995*, New York: Cushman & Wakefield of New York Reseach Services.

Danielson, M.N. and J.W. Doig, 1987, New York: *The Politics of Regional Development*, Berkeley CA: Univ. of California Press.

Dean, A.O. & A. Freeman, 1986. "The Rockefeller Center of the 80s?" *Architecture*, December.

Deane, Gary, 1992. Director, NYC Mayor's Office of Environmental Coordination, former Director of Planning BPCA. Interviewed by David Gordon, June 23.

Deutsche, R. 1991. "Uneven Development: Public Art in New York City," in Ghirardo, D. *Out of Site: A Social Criticism of Architecture*, Seattle: Bay Press.

Dixon, J.M. 1993. "The First 40 Years," *Progressive Architecture*, January, pp. 95–103.

Doubilet, S. 1986. "P/A Profile: Cooper Eckstut Associates," *Progressive Architecture*, July 1986, pp. 98–102.

Douglass, Robert, R. 1995. Chairman, DLMA; Former Secretary to Governor Nelson Rockefeller. Interviewed by David Gordon, July 26.

Downtown Express, 1994. "New South Park Design Gets Warmer Reception," *Downtown Express*, March 8, p. 4.

Downtown-Lower Manhattan Association, 1958. *Lower Manhattan: Recommended Land Use, Redevelopment Areas, Traffic Improvements*, New York: DLMA October 14. Consultants: Skidmore Owings & Merrill.

Downtown-Lower Manhattan Association 1963. *Lower Manhattan Major Improvements: Land Use, Transportation, Traffic*, New York: DLMA. November, Consultants: Skidmore Owings & Merrill.

Downtown-Lower Manhattan Association, 1973. *Fourth Report*, New York: DLMA. Consultant: Vollmer Associates.

Eckstut, S. 1986. "Solving Complex Urban Design Problems" in Fitzgerald, A.R. (ed.) *Waterfront Planning and Development*, New York: American Society of Civil Engineers, pp. 54–7.

Eckstut, Stanton, 1992. Architect and Urban Designer. Interviewed by David Gordon, June 16.

Eichenthal, David, R. 1990. "Changing Styles and Strategies of the Mayor" in Bellush & Netzer, *Urban Politics New York Style*, New York: Sharpe, pp. 63–85.

Elliot, Donald, 1986. Former Chairman CPC. Interviewed by Frederick Hayes, June 25.

Elliot, Donald, 1992. Former Chairman CPC. Interviewed by David Gordon, June 25.

Emil, David, 1992. BPCA President and CEO. Interviewed by David Gordon, June 29.

Fainstein, S.S. 1994. *The City Builders: Property, Politics & Planning in London and New York* Oxford UK: Basil Blackwell.

Fisher, T. 1988. "Building the New City" in *Progressive Architecture*, 3:88, pp. 86–93.

Foster, P. 1986. *The Master Builders: How the Reichmanns Reached for an Empire*, Toronto: Key Porter Books. Chapters 4–6.

Frucher, Meyer, S. 1992. Senior Vice President, Olympia & York, Former President BPCA. Interviewed by David Gordon, June 10.

Gill, B. 1990. "The Sky Line: Battery Park City" in *The New Yorker*, Aug. 20.

Goldberger, P. 1974. "Dispute Over Battery Park City Project Pits Architects vs. Planners vs. Developers," *New York Times*, November 26, p. 41.

Goldberger, P. 1983a. "The Year's Best: 1983 in Review," *New York Times*, December 25.

Goldberger, P. 1988. "To The Heights Of Simplicity," *New York Times Magazine*, November 20.

Goldberger, P. 1990. "Battery Park City's Brave New World," *Architectural Digest*, November, pp. 142–148.

Goldstein, Paul. 1992. District Manager, Manhattan Community Board #1. Interviewed by David Gordon, June 18.

Gordon, D.L.A. 1997a. "Managing The Changing Political Environment In Urban Waterfront Redevelopment," *Urban Studies*, Vol. 34, No. 1, pp. 61–83.

Gordon, D.L.A. 1997b. "Financing Urban Waterfront Redevelopment," *Journal of the American Planning Association*, Vol. 63, No. 2, pp. 244–265, forthcoming.

Gordon, D.L.A. 1996 "Planning, Design & Managing Change in Urban Waterfront Redevelopment," *Town Planning Review* (UK), Vol. 67, No. 3, pp. 261–290, July.

Hamilton, C.V. 1990. "Needed, More Foxes: The Black Experience" in Bellush & Netzer, *Urban Politics New York Style*, New York: Sharpe, pp. 359–384.

Harrison, W. 1966. *Battery Park City, New living space for New York*, New York: Harrison & Abramovitz Architects, February.

Hoelterhoff, M. 1988. "Bringing the Stroller Set to Battery Park City," *The Wall Street Journal*, July 14, p. 24.

Housing New York Corporation, 1987. *Revenue Bonds, 1987 Series A Official Statement*, New York: BPCA, October 1.

Howett, C. 1989. "Battery Park City," *Landscape Architecture*, May.

Hoyle, B.S., D.A. Pinder & M.S. Husain, 1988. *Revitalising the Waterfront: International Dimensions of Dockland Development*, London: Bellhaven.

Huxley, Tessa, 1992. Executive Director, Battery Park City Parks Corporation. Interviewed by David Gordon, June 19.

Huxtable, A.L. 1966a. "City Gets a Sweeping Plan for Rejuvenating Lower Manhattan," *New York Times*, June 22, p. 1.

Huxtable, A.L. 1966b. "City of Hope, Despair," *New York Times* June 26, p. 22D.

Huxtable, A.L. 1969. "Plan's 'Total' Concept is Hailed," *New York Times*, April 17.

Huxtable, A.L. 1979. "Is This the Last Chance for Battery Park City?" *New York Times*, November 7.

Huxtable, A.L. 1970. "Architecture: How Not to Build a City," *New York Times*, November 22.

Huxtable, A.L. 1981. "A New 'Rockefeller Center' Planned for Battery Park," *New York Times*, May 24.

Jacobs, Jane, 1961. *The Death and Life of Great American Cities*, New York: Vintage.

Jensen, Robert, 1969. "Battery Park City," *Architectural Record*, June, pp. 145–150.

Johnson, K. 1990. "Poetry & Public Service" in *Art in America*, March, pp. 161–4.

Johnson, Philip, 1992. Architect. Interviewed by David Gordon June 10.

Kahan, Richard, 1992. President, The Urban Assembly. Former Chairman, BPCA. Interviewed by David Gordon, June 16.

Kahan, Richard, 1995. President, The Urban Assembly. Former Chairman, BPCA. Interviewed by David Gordon, July 26.

Klapper, Byron, 1978. "Tax Exempts: New York's Battery Park City Authority in Lower Manhattan Is Facing Cash Woes," *Wall Street Journal*, December 4, p. 37.

Koch, Edward, 1992. Former Mayor, New York City. Interviewed by David Gordon, June 19.

Koenig, Peter, 1977. "Rocky Premises: Battery Park City Is an $80 Million Hole in the Ground," *Barron's*, April 18, p. 5.

Kozlowski, Thomas, 1992. Senior Director, BPCA. Interviewed by David Gordon, June 23.

Larson, K. 1985. "Combat Zone," *New York*, May 13, pp. 117–118.

Lindquist, Warren, L. 1995. Former VP DLMA and personal assistant to David Rockefeller. Telephone interview by David Gordon, July 17.

Lindsay, John, V. 1992. Former Mayor, New York City. Interviewed by David Gordon, June 25.

Marshall, Alton, 1986. Former Secretary to Governor Nelson Rockefeller. Interviewed by Frederick Hayes, July 16.

McHugh, C. 1991. "At Battery Park City, Brave New Garden Design Is Uprooted," *The New York Observer*, October 21.

McMillian, Jon, 1992. Director of Planning, BPCA. Interviewed by David Gordon, June 9.

Mitchell, J. & G.J. Miller, 1992. "Public Authorities and Contemporary Debt Financing," in Mitchell, J. (ed.), *Public Authorities and Public Policy: The Business of Government*, New York: Praeger.

Moss, M.L. 1976. "The Urban Port: A Hidden Resource for the City and the Coastal Zone," *Coastal Zone Management Journal*, Vol. 2, No. 3, pp. 223–245.

Moss, M.L. and M. Drennan, 1976. *The New York City Waterfront: An Analysis of Municipal Ownership and Leasing of Public Land*, New York: New York Sea Grant Report Series, NYU.

Moss, Mitchell, 1992. Director, New York University, Urban Research Center. Interviewed by David Gordon, June 10.

Netzer, Dick, 1990. "The Economy and Servicing of the City" in Bellush & Netzer, *Urban Politics New York Style*, New York: Sharpe, pp. 27–64.

New York City Department of City Planning, 1993a. *Plan For Lower Manhattan Waterfront*, October, NYC DCP 93–23.

New York City Department of City Planning, 1994. *Annual Report on Social Indicators*, NYC DCP 95–04.

New York City Department of Housing Preservation and Development, 1991. "Report on the Housing New York Program," New York: NYCHPD, December 31.

New York City Lower Manhattan Task Force, 1994. "A Plan for the Revitalization of Lower Manhattan," December 15.

New York City Office of Lower Manhattan Development, 1975. *Lower Manhattan Waterfront*, June.

New York City Planning Commision, 1969. "Battery Park City Master Plan Report," CP-20789, August 20.

New York City Planning Commission, 1964. *The Port of New York: Proposals for Development*. Comprehensive Planning Report. September.

New York State Budget Office, 1979. "Report: Battery Park City Authority" October 28.

New York State *General Laws 1968*, ch. 343.

New York State *General Laws 1969*, ch. 624.

New York State *General Laws 1971*, ch. 377.

New York State *General Laws 1976*, c.38.

Newhouse, V. 1989. *Wallace K. Harrison, Architect*, New York: Rizzoli.

Newman, Oscar, 1973. *Defensible Space: Crime Prevention Through Urban Design*, New York: Collier.

NYT, Abbreviation for *The New York Times*, Author's collection of 100+ articles, 1961–91.

Pitruzzello, Philip, R. 1995. BPCA President and CEO. Interviewed by David Gordon, July 25.

Plunz, R. 1990. *A History of Housing in New York City: Dwelling Type and Social Change in the American Metropolis*, New York: Columbia University Press.

Posner, E. 1989. "Battery Park City: An Island in Manhattan," *The Wall Street Journal*, January 5.

Progressive Architecture, 1966. "Back to the Waterfront: Chaos or Control?" *Progressive Architecture*, 47:8, pp. 128–139.

Progressive Architecture, 1995. "Lower Manhattan Plan: Award, Steven, K. Peterson," *Progressive Architecture*, January, pp. 68–71.

Rossant, James, S. 1992. Architect and Urban Designer. Interviewed by David Gordon, June 18.

Rowe, C. and F. Koetter 1978. *Collage City*, Cambridge MA: MIT Press.

Russell, F.P. 1994. "Battery Park City: An American Dream of Urbanism," in B. C. Scheer & W. Prieser (eds.) *Design Review: Challenging Urban Aesthetic Control*, New York: Chapman & Hall, pp. 197–209.

Sagalyn, L.B. 1992. "Public Development: Using Land as a Capital Resource," Cambridge MA: Lincoln Institute of Land Policy Working Paper Series.

Sagalyn, L.B. 1993. "Leasing: The Strategic Option for Public Development," Cambridge MA: Lincoln Institute of Land Policy Working Paper Series.

Serpico, Robert, 1992. Chief Financial Officer, BPCA. Interviewed by David Gordon, June 19.

Siroka, Martin, 1992. Vice President, New York City Housing Development Corporation. Interviewed by David Gordon, June 24.

Sorkin, M. (ed.) 1992. *Variations On A Theme Park: The New American City and the End of Public Space*, New York: Noonday Press.

Starr, Rodger, 1995. Contributing Editor, *City Journal*. Interviewed by David Gordon, July 20.

Starr, Roger, 1993. "A Stroll Through Battery Park City," *City Journal*, Vol. 3, No. 4, pp. 110–15. Autumn 1995.

Strickland, R. (ed.) 1991. *Between Edge and Fabric: Battery Park City*, New York: Columbia University, Graduate School of Architecture, Planning and Preservation. Catalog of exhibit held in the WFC July–September.

Time, 1990. "Best of the Decade," June 1, 1990, pp. 102–103.

Urstadt, Charles, J. 1992. Former Chairman and President, BPCA. Interviewed by David Gordon, June 15.

Vitullo-Martin, Julia, 1993. "The Livable City: Confronting the Quality of Life," *City Journal,* Vol 3, No. 4, Autumn, pp. 27–34.

Vollmer Associates, 1979. *A Reexamination of Battery Park City*, New York: Downtown Lower Manhattan Association, April 24.

Wade, Richard, C. 1990. "The Withering Away of the Party System" in Bellush & Netzer, *Urban Politics New York Style,* New York: Sharpe, pp. 271–295.

Wagner, Robert, F., Jr. 1992. Former Deputy Mayor, New York City and CPC Chairman. Interviewed by David Gordon, June 12.

Wallace, McHarg, Roberts, Todd, *et al.* 1965. *The Lower Manhattan Plan*, New York: New York City Planning Commission.

Walsh, A.H. 1990. "Public Authorities and the Shape of Decision Making" in Bellush & Netzer, *Urban Politics New York Style*, New York: Sharpe.

Whyte, W.H. 1988. *City: Rediscovering the Center*, New York: Bantam Doubleday Dell.

Wiseman, C. 1986. "The Next Great Place: The Triumph of Battery Park City" in *New York*, June 16, p. 34–41.

Wiseman, C. 1987. "A vision with a message" in *Architectural Record*, March, p. 113–121.

Wrubel, Arthur, 1995. Deputy Assistant Commissioner, NYC Department of Transportation. Interviewed by David Gordon, July 20.

APPENDIX

BATTERY PARK CITY CASH FLOW MODEL

	1969	1970	1971	1972	1973
INCOME					
PRIVATE INCOME					
PROPERTY REVENUE:					
Base Rent					
Supplemental Rent					
Condominium Sales Payment					
Other & Civic Facilities Payments					
PROPERTY REVENUE W/O PILOT	0	0	0	0	0
Payment In Lieu Of Taxes (PILOT)					
Sales Tax PILOT					
LESS PILOT to New York City					
NET PILOT RETAINED BY BPCA	0	0	0	0	0
TOTAL PROPERTY REVENUE	**0**	**0**	**0**	**0**	**0**
BOND & INTEREST INCOME:					
Private Start Up Loan	600				
Loan Repaid	(600)				
1972 Series A Bond Issue Proceeds				196,700	
LESS NYS Grants Repaid				(5,134)	
LESS Investment of Excess Cash From 1972 Issue				(189,858)	
Net Principal of Maturing Inv., Incl. Accrued Interest				725	16,519
1972 Series A Interest Income				1,403	10,773
LESS 1972 Series A Interest Expense					(12,429)
LESS 1972 Series A Principal Payments					
1980 Pod III Construction Loan Bonds Proceeds					
LESS Bond Issuance Cost					
Construction Loan Bonds Interest					
LESS Construction Loan Bonds Interest Expense					
LESS Construction Loan Bond Redemption					

Index